THE FLAG AND THE CROSS

National Limits and Church Universal

Bernard Thorogood

SCM PRESS LTD

British Library Cataloguing in Publication Data

Thorogood, Bernard
The flag and the cross: national limits
and Church universal.
1. Nationalism. Religious aspects
I. Title
291.1′77

ISBN 0-334-00490-X

100043060X

First published 1988
by SCM Press Ltd
26–30 Tottenham Road, London N1 4BZ

Typeset at The Spartan Press Ltd,
Lymington, Hants
and printed in Great Britain by
Richard Clay Ltd,
Bungay, Suffolk

THE FLAG AND THE CROSS

CONTENTS

Introduction   vii

One · Dynamo or Demon?   1

Two · Tribal Blessings   5

Three · Breaking the Mould   14

Four · Courage and Compromise   21

Five · British Ambiguities   33

Six · The National Church   41

Seven · Minority Churches   50

Eight · Patriotism and Protest   58

Nine · The World Parish   66

Ten · Nation, Church, Kingdom   76

Note on Ethnic Churches   86

A name, but not Babel   88

INTRODUCTION

Throughout its history, the Christian church has had an uneasy relationship with the national or imperial units into which humanity has been divided. Sometimes Christians have appeared as the sponsors, clients, supporters, recipients or close allies of the authorities, as hearty patriots ready to bless the flag. But at other times Christians have seemed to have little regard for the nationalism which grips so many. They have appeared to be people with a contrary view of the true nature of the state, or people with an international identity. This is still puzzling for many of us. We cannot easily escape from the very great pressure of national sentiment. Should we even try to do so? Are we called by God to be defenders of a nation? Is that a meaning of the title Defender of the Faith?

We are also puzzled by the shape of church life in the United Kingdom, with our varied histories which make it so hard to plan or to achieve any major new pattern for a new age. When a church belongs, in some sense, to the nation, who can give it freedom to follow conscience? Is it trapped?

And I find it necessary to ask whether our present nation states – with all their influence on the shape of church life – are in any sense the final destiny of human community. Are we as Christians called to point the way forward to a broader and also a more local authority in economic and political life? Has our rather thoughtless acceptance of the nation state helped to retain war as an instrument of policy?

These are the questions which have caused me to write, to provide a basis for a discussion which no doubt will carry this issue into many areas of theology which are beyond my reach.

CHAPTER ONE

Dynamo or Demon?

No power in the modern world has so Janus-like a face as nationalism. It is a plague, a disease which intermittently runs riot in the blood of society, destroying good sense, rationality, tolerance, charity and even humanity itself. It is stirred up by war and is the cause of war. It makes fantastic claims, so that our nationality becomes more important than our membership of the one human community. Nationalism pervades our thought so that, without intention, we categorize and label each national population, assuming that the features we most dislike are common to all. Nationalism corrupts some very fine human qualities so that courage becomes arrogance and love becomes exclusiveness. It can become so powerful a net that it traps education, art, sport, morals and faith, reducing them all to the level of tools of the state.

But there is another face. We cannot ignore the great advances in human life which have resulted from the energies of nationalism. In places of very mixed population, such as the United States, national- ism has enabled a sense of common purpose to bind people together, so that immigrant communities can catch a common vision. To nationalism we owe some of the great achievements of architecture and language, of exploration and research. The creation of the modern democratic system, the application of vast economic re- sources and the preservation of a cultural inheritance all owe much to this strange spirit of nationhood.

Such a bifocal reality has always presented Christian faith with a difficult challenge. Flag-waving Christians have been very common. Indeed, it can be argued that the incentive for the modern nation state came in part from those Christian leaders who had a vision of national churches in the period between Wycliffe and Luther and Knox. Certainly Christians have led the imperial expansion of nations without any sense of religious constraint – Portugal and Spain,

Holland, France and Britain can all record people of faith who carried both cross and national flag across the world. Has this been a massive compromise of Christian faith? Or has the faith so cleansed our nationalism as to render it harmless?

It is not a simple question, and the answers we reach may well depend on our personal experience or on the period of history with which we are familiar, or on our ethical stance on war or on the stage of development of the nation where we are at home. But it is an important question. Like it or not we all live in a nation state where loyalty and patriotism are expected of us. From the nation state we derive great benefits, which we accept as rights, such as personal security and the security of property, streets and water and sewage, schools and a fire service, and so many more. We are citizens, with all that this implies for both rights and duties. We are never wholly at one with all the policies of the nation, which we recognize are always a compromise and which may ignore what we regard as of first importance, yet this disagreement does not cancel our sense of belonging, nor our citizenship duties. We just cannot evade our nationality. To become stateless is the dream of a very few protesters and I do not think that this has any real effect on the patterns of human society. But we are also Christians who recognize a citizenship which God has given us through faith in Christ. We belong to him through creation and redemption. His law of life has become our guide and the cross has become the sign of the Kingdom. So we are constantly confronted with claims upon us which belong to the ultimate, absolute being of God.

The coming together of these two claims is today more crucial than ever because of the vast power of the modern nation. Ideology, law, trade, education and military might make up a terrifying combination from which we are unable to escape. Even the smaller nations today have greater power because of the means of communication which enable them to appeal to the world and, if they wish, replace reality with propaganda. But it is the enormity of the nuclear arsenal which really makes us discuss this issue. There is not much to choose between the terrors of an Assyrian attack on Jerusalem three thousand years ago and an Iranian assault on Iraq today. Death smells the same in Vietnam and at Waterloo. Our consciousness is moved by the modern possibility of total mass death which can also render the earth poisoned for generations to come. A nationalism which regards such a possibility as some kind of shield, a threat which could one day become reality, causes us to examine the claims of nation and faith anew.

There are two other pressures on us to face the whole issue. One is the vast changes in our own nation over the last thirty years, which make any pretence of being a Christian nation very dubious. The population has become permanently diversified by racial, cultural and religious mixtures. This is the most significant social change in my lifetime. It has brought into our national life major groups of people who are devoted to other faith disciplines, and just as the Jewish presence led towards toleration laws in the nineteenth century, so the life of other faiths today calls into question any easy identity of nation and church. Toleration is not now the issue, for the legal rights question has been settled. What is very much at issue is the lingering assumption of both state and Christians that the nation is a Christian creation, with a special place in God's love, and with archbishop and sovereign as partners in leadership responsibility. Such assumptions (probably more common among non-practising Christians than active church attenders) hinder any real attempt to assess the character of church and nation. They stifle any radical Christianity. Yet they provide a residual base-line of religious feeling which could be a starting point for growth. How do people of other faiths experience this nominal alliance? It has been noted that in India the Christian minority has always rejoiced in the secularization of the state, as the only defence against an overwhelming Hindu power. So it would be healthy for Christians in Britain to discover the thinking of our minorities here.

The other major influence surrounding this issue is the internationalism which affects all our lives and which is now an unalterable factor in the church. No nation now lives on its own, not even the mammoths. The ancient Chinese vision of the 'middle kingdom' which could effectively wall itself around and so prevent contamination has disappeared with international travel, international science, the race for unclaimed resources in the oceans, the war games which ignore frontiers, the youth culture, the power contests of the great powers. It is significant that the great international meetings, such as the United Nations or the Olympic Games, provide a forum for acute nationalism, for it is precisely when the autonomy of the nation state is threatened that it becomes most vocal and vigorous. The European Community is another example. This modest advance towards transnational organization and decision-making is met by the up-thrust spikes of national vetoes, the cries of national warriors and the vague antipathy of many citizens. Quietly, however, international influences have their way, as the weekend shopping basket testifies, and there is an erosion of national autonomy.

Is it so – or is it to become so – in the church? Is the international church the coming sign of the reign of God, as Catholicism has signified through the centuries? Were the churches of the Reformation weak in their acceptance of national synods and then national separation? But having entered into autonomous life as national churches, how do we now approach an internationalism which does not dominate but serves, and which resists the very human tendency to put organization in the place of spiritual life?

Perhaps Janus is the wrong image. Nationalism does not look to the past years with one face and to the future with another. It is closer to the masks of comedy and tragedy in the theatre. Nationalism wears the smile of human surprises, human oddity and diversity, it is part of the *comédie humaine*. But it also wears the ghastly face of horror, the medieval tragedy of blood. And faith sees both these faces. In Christ we are still citizens in this place, surrounded by the compromises of a democratic society and not absolutists. So we participate and wear our national dress. We belong. That is our privilege and our pain, shame and glory all mixed together in a jumble of history, in which we have to live out our pilgrimage. When Herbert Butterfield wrote that famous dictum, 'Hold to Christ, and for the rest be totally uncommitted,' he was speaking to the idealism which is every disciple's prayer. He was not addressing us in those commitments which are vital for corporate life. Only Simeon Stylites could fulfil that command and even he was heavily committed to the top of the pillar. We are caught in one commitment after another and the nation is there, among the voices, the holder of power, a tyrant-mother in the home and a question mark placed beside our faith.

CHAPTER TWO

Tribal Blessings

When we push back into our beginnings as a people – whichever part of the world we inhabit – we find ourselves in the culture and organization of the tribe. Defence against attackers, comrades in the hunt, contenders with natural disaster, builders of the walls, were all necessary for human life in many tough contexts. The early social organism, in a relatively empty world, was often an isolated tribe owing little to commerce and needing no adventure. In such a stable context the tradition of the tribe, its language and its gods, could appear permanent. But total isolation was rare. It persisted in some places into the modern age, as we find in New Guinea and parts of the upper Amazon basin. The mountain valley was the setting for most of these isolated tribes, for the journey across the mountain was an unnecessary labour into danger. In the more traversible country and on the borders of the oceans tribe bumped into tribe, power was disputed and the purity of language was broken.

That is where the religious question begins. If the gods belong to the tribe, then are all the tribes equally endowed? Is there any pecking order of the gods? Can the faith of this enclave be totally distinct from that? And what happens if we move from this oasis to the next, from this island to the next – do we have to learn a new pantheon and forget the old? In many places the religious question was hidden beneath that of political authority. When one tribe became dominant through battle or barter it imposed its gods, or they were widely accepted, as part of the cultural and linguistic dominance. The defeated gods became first the underground worship of a few and then the buried artefacts under the midden. But the more human contact was possible, the more pressing was the religious question. Who is god in this place? How do I worship him?

It is in this area of human life that we recognize the anguish and the particular contribution of the early parts of the Old Testament. The tribal characteristics were plain: there was the father of the clan, Abraham, before whom all was legend; a distinctive dialect; a nomadic life appropriate to the edges of the desert. But from those beginnings it is also clear that the deity of this tribe was jealous even in defeat, so that he could not be surrendered like a regimental banner. He remained the Lord for Israel even when Israel fell under another overlord. This was the meaning of 'jealous', which has an entirely unworthy ring in our ears. It was a key word for the people of Israel, and to it we owe the distinctiveness of their monotheism. Yahweh was never to be accommodated on the shelf with all the others. Egypt might have powerful deities; that could hardly be denied when the Nile rose in flood or the Pharaoh appeared in white and gold at the head of a great army. Assimilation was the easy and obvious way. It was the way to follow if an easy life were the objective. So the toughness of heart and mind which pledged loyalty to Yahweh alone was an exceptional gift.

For a nomadic people this was an essential dimension for their identity and independence. There were long periods when political independence was impossible and then the independence of faith, the turning to Yahweh in prayer, the trust in his authority were keystones for future life. The saga of Joseph is a reminder to all succeeding generations that even when the overlords are in control in the land there is assurance in the particular way of faith of the tribe of Israel. By subtlety or by wisdom, by miracle or by persuasion, by dreams or by disasters the God of Israel opens a door for his people. They belong to him. But, in a sense, he belongs to them. Yahweh is the Lord God of Abraham and Isaac in that he is related to them in a fashion unique in all the world. No one else knows him as this tribe knows him. So loyalty to the tribe and loyalty to its God were part of the same bundle of a way of life.

Within the Old Testament we see the tensions created by this tribal faith. The greatest evidence of the blessing of God was the release from captivity in Egypt, forever the model of divine deliverance. But the religious question pressed hard. Could the Lord, who was plainly with them in Egypt at that moment, also be with them in other places at other times? Or would he be left behind, to be replaced by a human leader and lord? This struggle of faith lies behind the exodus narrative. The presence of the Lord has to be demonstrated and the pillars of cloud and fire mark that presence, always a distance beyond, while the provision of water and food in the barren Sinai peninsula reveals a constant care. Most wonderful for the development of faith was the mountain of the Lord. The tribe had no settled base. There were no permanent markers to tell of the holy place for worship, as was the case for most tribal deities. The Lord was a wandering god. But through the revealing of himself at Sinai the people had a sanctuary, a name, by which they could speak of God. The implications of Sinai are remarkable. First, it was not the centre of a territory which the people could occupy. They were, in fact, to turn their backs on that location in order to find a land where they could settle. Second, it was not a place to erect a temple. There was no point in carrying stones up a hill which was itself just a monstrous jumble of stones. Third, it was not a place of sacrifice, and when the people attempted to create a typical temple statue they met the most powerful blast of opposition from their leader.

So the keynotes of this tribal faith were set in the desert. The first was mystery. Such strange powers had been revealed in the exodus that faith could never explain them, only accept and adore. God had been active in their lives. But his action was his choice. The tribe had not built up the powers of their god as a witch doctor might do by constantly adding new recipes and claiming new cures. Unexpectedly, action had saved them as a people, out of the blue. So the demand of God upon them, reaching them through the mouth of Moses, was a word from the cloud on the mountain, the invisible, the unnamed. Action was the second key. God, whose face was unknown, was revealed in what he did in the world, in the lives of men and women. 'I will be what I will be' could be understood as 'I will be what I will do'. Much tribal religion would have made a similar claim in many parts of the world. 'We prayed and rain came.' 'We made sacrifices and were victorious in the battle.' Such experience is often cited as evidence. The evidence in the Old Testament is remarkable because the activity of God results in the tribe being freed to become a nation, and the tribe being led into a morality that affirms the character of God. For morality is the third key. However much the detail of the ceremonial law in the Pentateuch was the work of later generations, there remains a body of ethical precept which quite plainly establishes the major values of society. The care for life itself, the principle of fairness in human dealings, the honour for the father of the family, essential hygiene, the best of all produce as an offering to God – so faith and daily life were bound inextricably together.

But in calling this a tribal faith I am pressing the point that at this very early stage the boundary drawn around the tribe was also the boundary drawn around faith. Yahweh was not seen as the god of the Egyptians or the Canaanites. They had their own gods. Yahweh was over-against them. He had selected his own people to whom he would listen and they must talk with him and no other. This tribal limitation turned brutal in the period we know as that of the Judges. Entry into a land which was rich enough for pastoral settlement meant a furious struggle for power, and the invading tribe required not only divine aid but tactical skills, much courage and, dare we say, a slice of luck. It is at this point that modern Christians have great difficulty with the biblical record. Is it possible that the God whom we know in the life of Christ was the God who ordered the devastation of cities and the wholesale slaughter of the people? We cannot hold this together in our faith. We *can* see it as the development of a tribal faith when confronted by the other tribes in a disputed territory. It was one stage in human growth to believe that the tribal god was bound to be a god of battles who rejoiced in the defeat of the enemy, and though this is not our perception we must admit that the tribal emphasis is not far under our skin. It is not far from chauvinism to believe that god is chauvinist too.

To occupy the land, however frightful the process, was the prologue to the story of a nation. Being settled, accepting boundaries, deciding land ownership, organizing the sub-tribes and finally establishing a capital city, led to the concept of a national life, a concept made visible in the throne. At that point the Israelite nation, though small on the world scene, had the major elements of national identity. Nation and faith were bound together.

This meant a long and sustained campaign against all the remains of other religious systems which had existed in the land. The jealousy of Yahweh was reaffirmed. The hilltop shrines – and the land is a mass of hills – were all suspect as centres of idolatry. Marriage with foreigners had to be strictly controlled, for that could be an area of leakage. Leadership in worship was regulated through the tribe of Levi so that there would be a permanent understanding of the religious law within that extended family. All this was emphasizing the unity of the nation in the unity of its faith. It was, and remains, a very powerful combination. The final symbol of it was the building of the temple and the suppression of all sacrifice elsewhere in the land. The centralizers won. Regulation, supervision, law and order triumphed over the haphazard local celebration. The glory of God and the glory of the nation came together at the temple and it was thus a focus of national feeling, the place to which all visitors came in wonder. The mystery of Sinai had become a curtain before the holiest shrine, and the place of sacrifice which combined passionate prayer with pious extortion.

Once the nation was established and the faith centralized, the basic religious question shifted into another gear. As a wandering tribe with its own god, there was room for the possibility that every tribe was so equipped. Each could be self-contained. But the nation which constantly had to deal with other nations and which praised Yahweh as the supreme authority over kings and which saw very powerful armies just over the horizon had to face the likelihood that Yahweh was in some strange way related to others as well. There were various possibilities. If God had created all humanity then he could be the same who was worshipped by other peoples by other names. All faiths could be inspired by the one giver of life. Or the Israelite people could be the only one on earth to be living and worshipping the truth, while all others were in darkness for ever. Or the light given to Israel could be the first candle from which others would catch light; there could be an 'infection' of truth. Or the other nations could be destined to become in some manner Israelite and lose their pagan identity. Or the Israelite faith could itself be in a development process, needing some aspects of reality present elsewhere in the world. Looking back from a rather comfortable distance we can see that the choice was never easy, that it involved tensions, that the tribes could be torn apart and that the outcome was a victory for a small, tough-minded group with tremendous loyalty but of doubtful charity.

For the conclusion which became dominant was that this one nation knew the meaning of true faith, and that although all other faiths were in some sense bogus, individuals could reach towards the living God by adopting the whole ritual of worship. The nation could attract, could teach, but could never relax. It is no wonder that the prophetic voices were unpopular. When Amos listed the sins of the surrounding nations and ended the list with very similar sins in Judah and Israel, he appeared to be placing everyone on the same level. When he declared, '"Are you not like the Ethiopians to me?" says the Lord,' the question may have seemed rhetorical, with the answer, 'Of course not.' But Amos, just a country preacher, was reaching out beyond the boundaries of the nation and saw the calling of God to all humanity and the purpose of God as justice throughout the earth. This was perhaps the first hint of a supra-national faith.

The same broad vision was powerfully expressed in the early part of Isaiah. In a parable form he was able to describe Israel in the traditional terms of God's special vineyard, the loved one, the place of fruitfulness and peace. But he turned the picture upside down with the declaration that no good fruit came from these vines so it would become a desolate place, useless to the landowner and only fit to be handed over to other gardeners (Isa. 5.1–7). This was an assault on the national image and in modern terms the worst of public relations. Isaiah was still speaking in terms of national faith but saw it betrayed

9

by the very way of life developing in Israel. Jeremiah saw the doom even closer and declared it in ways that could have been regarded as treason. Israel could not claim the blessing of national security in the arms of Yahweh while faith and life betrayed the covenant of the desert. In these pre-exile prophetic speeches the 'special relationship' is still there. It has not become a universal relationship. But the failures of Israel are seen to prevent the blessings that God longs to give them. In modern terms we might say, 'This splendid people and this lovely land have been given the most gracious gifts of God. He has showered us with talents. But what have we done with them? Our national life is such a totally corrupted mess, so shamelessly throwing away its ideals that tragedy is bound to come. It is very close, no further away than the next downturn of the economic spiral.'

When the tragedy happened the religious question pressed hard. If Babylon was stronger than Yahweh, who was god across the desert? When the nation was transported into subjection, would the Lord God go with them, or would he be only a dream of the old and a tale for the young? Just because of the temple focus in Jerusalem this question must have been all the harder to meet. With that gone to ruin, where could the people look? It was at this nadir of national fortune that religious inspiration came, a brimming cup of grace. Quite unpredictably the preachers raised the spiritual hope of Israel, not in the conventional way of a military revenge but by enlarging the horizons of faith. Ezekiel, in his visions, declared that God moved with and ahead of his people so that he was as truly present in Babylon as in Jerusalem. Wings and wheels were characteristics of the ever-present Lord (Ezek. 1 and 11.22–25). The prophet used the image of trees to represent the nations, with the noble cedar, the lord of the forest, as Assyria to be brought low while the little tree would grow tall (Ezek. 17.22–24 and 31.3–9). He preached with great clarity that the scattered people would be reunited: 'I am gathering up the Israelites from their places of exile among the nations; I will assemble them from every quarter and restore them to their own soil. I will make them one single nation in the land, on the mountains of Israel, and they shall have one king' (Ezek. 37.21–22). This was to be the coming together of the dry bones into a fresh, living, vigorous people (Ezek. 37.1–14). So the vision of a restored temple provides the new focus to replace the old. Ezekiel was thus able to do for the exiled people what Moses had done long ago in Egypt, to recognize the authority of God both in punishment and in restoration, an authority which spanned the extent of the known world and could work through the events of history.

Yet the national purpose, in Ezekiel, remains traditional. Whether or not we spiritualize the visions of the temple, that is where the covenant is to be celebrated, at the centre of national life. The prophet we know as Second Isaiah, or Isaiah of the Sufferings, was enabled to go much further. He could see that God had great purposes for this small nation – 'The Lord . . . formed me in the womb to be his servant' (Isa. 49.5), and that these purposes extended far beyond the geographical area of the land to the coasts and islands at the end of the earth, but that the work of God could only be fulfilled through suffering. God – the same God who loved Israel – worked through the enemy, 'Cyrus his anointed', and not only through those who worshipped at Jerusalem. We have the sense of a radical change in the concept of nationhood. If Israel is to be special, it is because this people has a service to perform for the whole world, a service which means humility and pain, not glory and banners and gold.

But such a radical vision of national purpose met an opposite response which is recorded for us in Ezra and Nehemiah. Out of exile is the theme, but the purpose is to draw the boundaries of Israel tighter than ever, to build the walls higher, to shut the city gates, to purify the ethnic stock, to re-establish central control of religion. How else, we may ask, can a tiny nation hold its place in the world? The failure, when we compare the vision of the servant people, was to envisage the nation in precisely the terms of popular nationhood. Because faith and politics were wrapped up together in one parcel, the narrowing of political aims was reflected in a nationalistic religious outlook. Defence was the key reaction, defence of the state and of the pure faith. But it is impossible for a small people to defend a world faith; it can defend a tribal faith. This became a testing matter again in the later period when Greek power, ideas, language and social patterns became so potent throughout the Mediterranean. Jews with courage and faith defended to the death, even when it meant retreating into the desert areas, for cohabitation was both treason and blasphemy. Yahweh and the pantheon were mutually exclusive. Even so, there grew an attraction in such a bold, stiff-necked religion which could sustain poor people in great trials. So the Jews found it necessary to learn both how to live faithfully in other lands and how to receive worshippers from other ethnic and cultural backgrounds. The pathway was the law, elaborated through the centuries, prescribing in detail the conduct and ritual necessary for cleansing before God. It offered a way by which non-Jews could ally themselves with the faith and so enter into the covenant – though some would have said that non-Jews always entered as second-class citizens, a mere shadow, never to be confused with the real thing.

To write in this way of the tribal religion as it developed and was challenged illuminates some of the features of Judaism when it met Jesus of Nazareth. But it misses a vital constituent. From the earliest period and through to the days of Roman occupation the faith had vast dimensions. The Lord God of Hosts who created the earth, who called the stars onto parade by number, who set sun and moon in their daily circulation, who gave life to leviathan in the depths, who beat out the vault of the skies, and who breathed the breath of life into the human frame, this God could not be said to be made in the image of man. Even the summit of Sinai amid the thunder was only a tiny glimpse of the power of God. So faith meant wonder, adoration, worship. No 'graven image' was possible, for the human imagination which creates an image can never present God as though he is a Martian to be visualized, and the presence of God can never be reduced to what itself has no life. The greatness of so early an appreciation of the otherness of God is surely our constant ground for thanksgiving.

But was that, too, a typically tribal approach, to elevate the tribe by singing the praises of its god? After all, what tribe in a struggle for power would ever say, 'Our god is a small domestic deity who can only command this one square mile of territory'? I think the clearest indication that this faith was not simply a projection is that the vision of God in the Old Testament was never reduced by the defeat and subjection of the believers. The greatest vision of God was not in the days of Solomon, as a heavenly reflection of an earthly throne, but in the days of exile when, by all pragmatic tests the God of Israel had no power at all. We can contrast this with the pantheons of Greece and Rome. Their scope and wonder in human consciousness dwindled with the political decline, though Greeks and Romans struggled to retain a minimal respect for the shrines. I am constrained to say that this constant faith in Israel's transcendent God who was before our beginnings and who will be beyond our end was not a manufacture but a gift.

Such a God bound to such a tribe is the very stuff of nationalism. Holding such a precious gift but in so vulnerable a context, believing that this mighty God had made a personal selection of this hard people, there was no possibility of a relaxed relationship with the surrounding powers. Israel, a nation of faith, stood against the world. To be a faithful son of Abraham meant both to worship according to the law and to defend the corporate life. Something of this potent combination has been retained in the modern state of Israel, to the confusion of all logical statesmen and as a threat to unbelievers in the midst. That vision of the suffering servant, so hopeful for a humble, evangelical, non-imperial presence was lost in the fury of the Maccabean revolt and translated into the agony of a lost kingdom at Massada. When God has to be defended by swords, a species of idolatry has begun. Of course it may be said that throughout Jewish history it was the nation and not the faith which was at risk, but the two were so intimately entangled that it is not possible now to separate them at the crisis times.

Such a crisis, a point of judgment, was the appearance of the preacher of Nazareth.

CHAPTER THREE

Breaking the Mould

King Herod had good cause to be worried. A star-crowned baby at historic Bethlehem, of the tribe and lineage of David, sought by foreign professors and announced by wild-eyed shepherds – this could indeed be another threat to the throne. So many hopes were directed towards a national saviour who would restore Israel's glory that any mention of 'future king' was enlarged into a dramatic divine intervention. God's anointed one would be more than king, he would also be healer, teacher, priest. But in the life and work of Jesus we see a refusal to fit the national hope. He transcended it because it would imprison the salvation coming from God. Yet Jesus was fully a man of his nation, at one with his contemporaries. It is this mixture of identification with Israel and refusal to accede to Israel's hopes that broke the mould of national faith.

We see this at the very start of the ministry of Jesus when he rejected the possibility of political dominance as a way of salvation. How much could have been achieved, with Jesus on the throne of a new empire! But what a betrayal it would have been of the Kingdom of God! The reign of Jesus would have been limited by space and time, by the compromises of all social life and by the enforcement in law of God's way of love. Another Moses with a finer decalogue was not a saviour. Yet with every healing and wonderful act the temptation must have continued. 'Jesus, aware that they meant to come and seize him to proclaim him king, withdrew again to the hills by himself' (John 6.15). The risk of popularity was great. It might have created a national hero at any moment in those years of the ministry, but Jesus was aware that this was a testing of his obedience to the true vocation. At the end the Jewish authorities could find no ground for the execution they needed other than a treasonable claim to be king, and this is how they presented the case to the Roman governor. 'Are you a king then?' asked Pilate. Jesus answered, '"King" is your word.' It was the word a politician could deal with. 'Jesus of Nazareth, King of the Jews' became the ironic label on a criminal's cross, the end of a popular dream. So Jesus rejected one way to a kingdom.

But of greater significance for us is the very life and attitude of Jesus as it touched the national hope and the national prejudice. Towards the hope he was negative. He did not see a period of strength and prosperity ahead for the Jewish people. He saw no relief from the Roman overlords but only greater strife ahead. Jerusalem was not destined for glory as the great national shrine, but for destruction, ruin and death. Jesus did not teach opposition to the Romans as many Jews might have hoped. Pay the Roman taxes, go with the officer two miles when he compels you for one. Jesus was ready to mix with those who fraternized with Rome and could say of a Roman centurion, 'I tell you, nowhere, even in Israel, have I found faith like this' (Luke 7.9). So the hope of a great national revival seems to have had no place in his thought. He was equally dismissive of the national prejudice, the xenophobia which had so long been a defensive wall. A Samaritan became the model of the good neighbour, and a Samaritan woman was a serious questioner who deserved the full attention of Jesus. One of the most ancient barriers was broken. In dealing with the Phoenician woman from Syria (Mark 7.24–30) Jesus declared that the message was first of all for those prepared through the ancient covenant, but went on to react warmly to her trust and gave fresh life to an obsessed child. There is in these contacts something of the open spirit of the story of Ruth who came from Moab but offered faithfulness greater than was found in Israel. Jesus cared for people too much to be concerned with the labels of nationality.

Even more radical was his attitude towards the national focus of worship in Jerusalem. That he was a worshipper, we know. He went up to the feasts and it is plain that Tabernacles and Passover meant much to him. He honoured the temple to the extent that he was appalled at its desecration and misuse by the commercial hangers-on. Yet he could say to the woman of Samaria that 'the time is coming when you will worship the Father neither on this mountain, nor in Jerusalem . . . the time approaches, indeed it is already here, when those who are real worshippers will worship the Father in spirit and in truth' (John 4.21–23). To this we may link the saying in Matthew, 'For where two or three have met together in my name, I am there among them' (Matt. 18.20). This is a moment of liberation for human history, release from the limitations of the shrine so that true worship is possible everywhere. It is not simply a preference for the synagogue over against the temple. A host of dispersed Jews had no opportunity

15

to visit Jerusalem regularly and for them the synagogue was the essential place of worship. Jesus did more than commend dispersion. He actually removed from the concept of worship that attachment to a building which had lasted from the primitive days of stone circles and rough pyramids. Since the temple was the national shrine as well as a holy place, this meant a deep review of national life, pride and history; and for this the official guardians of formal religion could not forgive him.

As he was leaving the temple one of his disciples exclaimed, 'Look, Master, what huge stones! What fine buildings!' Jesus said to him, 'You see these great buildings? Not one stone will be left upon another; all will be thrown down' (Mark 13.1–2).

Yet worship in its truest sense would continue. The Father could be approached by his children anywhere and neither the building, nor the city, nor the nation were essential ingredients. Christian disciples do not need to weep at the wall of a lost temple. Yet the attachment of faith to a building remains with people of all faiths and is not easily set beside belief in the heavenly city. We are mostly paradoxical people, protesting that we worship in spirit, have no need of images, travel through life as pilgrims with Christ, yet when our particular building is threatened with dry rot or the planning authorities are pushing a new road through the church property, then we stick fast to our stones like barnacles on a ship's hull. The purpose is freedom – for the believer to meet the Lord, for the Lord to feed his people, for our needs to be expressed – and for this purpose Jesus was prepared to face all the strength of the opposition.

That opposition reached its climax at the cross. Many elements contributed to this act of rejection, and not all can be called political panic. There was, for example, the outsider quality of Jesus; he was not a product of the temple schools, not from a leading family, not grey-haired, but with a provincial accent and a rough group of friends. So when such a one became popular, the immediate reaction was to dismiss him for ever. Again, there was his extraordinary familiarity with God. The official guardians of religion had always been trained to think of God as unapproachable, too holy to speak his name, so that the outer courts were the proper place for ordinary people. But Jesus addressed God simply as Father and proclaimed that easy approach for all. To some this was blasphemous, and there may have been sincerely troubled minds that took that view. To others there was a threat to all professional religion. If the simple person could simply seek the forgiveness of God, confident that God hears as readily as a loving father, then those who tended the elaborate liturgy of the temple would be superfluous. All this was additional to the political argument. Under Rome any local uprising was a risk for the whole population, for martial law reduced the few national freedoms. A popular movement, crowds to hear an orator, wonders of healing, and all based up north in Galilee – that was a risk to the status quo and deserved severe treatment.

It has often been claimed, particularly by Jewish scholars, that the teaching of Jesus was not original and that the roots of all his major thoughts are in the Old Testament. I believe that in a strictly textual sense this is true. We can trace the background of many of the sayings, particularly to the Psalms and the prophetic books. But that is not to say that Jesus was repeating the message of former preachers. If he had been, the reaction would not have been so violent. He gave a quite fresh meaning to old words, a new emphasis and hope. For example, the address to God as Father can be traced to verses such as Psalm 103.13, 'As a father has compassion on his children, so has the Lord compassion on all who fear him' or to Isaiah 9.6 where a messianic title is Everlasting Father. But the use of the word by Jesus is on quite a different basis. It is not the occasional metaphor. It is the constant, familiar address, the central way of approach. Another example is the way of forgiveness. It is familiar enough in the Old Testament that prayer to God for forgiveness is real. We have only to read Psalm 51 to appreciate the depth of this pleading for release. In the gospels, however, forgiveness becomes a present reality; it is here and now in the person of Jesus and is to be the pattern of relationship among his followers. The roots indeed are old. The fruit is new.

This newness was most dramatic and radical when Jesus said, 'For even the Son of Man did not come to be served but to serve, and to give up his life as a ransom for many' (Mark 10.45). The life became the offering. So, as the writer to the Hebrews taught, a whole history of the sacrificial system came to its conclusion. What had been a narrow way of awesome religious satisfaction, an elaborate ritual of deep meaning for some, met the self-offering of the Lamb of God. The doorway was opened. All could see, acknowledge, tremble, trust before the cross. Mark gives the word to the centurion, a word which the disciples found hard to express, 'Truly this man was a son of God.' The historical roots of such self-offering may be traced to Isaiah 53. But to translate that song of the sufferer into actual rejection, into final pain, and to go that way because it was obedience to love, and to go that way when the treasury of divine power was available, and to go that way right to the end, even though it looked like failure and solitude – that was beyond all expectation and explanation.

The mould, like the tomb, was finally broken by Easter. Nothing had prepared Israel for such a climax and ever since the Jewish people have been at a loss in dealing with the event. It is too outlandish, and to accept it leads to a conviction about the nature of Christ which does not match the national Messiah hope. For the risen and ascended Christ is freed from all the limitations of culture, language, time and geography. 'I am with you always, to the end of time' and wherever you go, is the promise. All nations, in Matthew's version, are to be brought into discipleship and, in Luke, the disciples are sent to the ends of the earth (Acts 1.8). So the mission of Jesus Christ which had so narrow a frame, so local a reference, was made universal. The breadth of God's action was revealed. It was the transformation of tribal and national hope to become a world faith for a world restored to its maker.

The pressures to keep this gift within the old limitations were very great. People who had been trained through a millennium of national history to regard the chosen people as a national entity and to cherish the purity of that enclave in a wicked world could not easily shake off the national habit. Appreciation of what God had done in Christ came with a loss of old certainties. That Rome should have rejected Jesus Christ and finally carried out his execution was not a surprise, for that was the way of a cruelly indifferent imperial philosophy. The shock was that Israel should, in large measure, have also rejected him. That shock was the climax of the address of Peter at Pentecost (Acts 2.36) and of the defence of Stephen before the council (Acts 7.52). It was a profound theological issue for Paul as we see in the letter to the Romans. The greatest test of the immediate followers of Jesus was whether they could translate the world saviour into a world faith or whether they would narrow his calling, restrict his promises and seek to provide a renewed impetus to Judaism.

The issue was decided by four main factors. First was the Pentecost gift of the Spirit, bringing a new dynamism, courage and hope. The gathering of so many different groups in Jerusalem testifies to the drawing power of the temple tradition, but the gift of languages at Pentecost is recorded as a sign of the universality of the church. Pentecost was thus a new beginning, confirming all that the risen Christ had promised. Second was the determined opposition of the Jewish authorities. This first persecution of Christians in defence of the traditional priesthood compelled the apostles to move outwards from Jerusalem with no prospect of a new synthesis. The third factor was the two conversions – that of Peter at Joppa and that of Paul on the way to Damascus. Both meant radical change, in the one case to a full acceptance of gentile Christians, and in the other to a life in Christ wherever he might lead. Fourth came the Council at Jerusalem recorded in Acts 15, when the results of early missionary work were tested. It was the last point at which the old parameters could have been enforced. The law of Israel's life could have been imposed. But the breadth of the Gospel had become plain, and those with first-hand experience of the gentile mission could never go back to the old concept of proselytes to Judaism.

It is hard for us to appreciate the critical nature of this outward movement for the early disciples. It was indeed, in Pascal's terms, a wager, betting on God, putting all at risk with no road back into the security of the Jewish law. Some ambivalence remained. Respect for the temple was not easily abandoned, and for some years Jerusalem seemed the natural focus, the birthplace of the church. The vexed question of food which had been blessed in a pagan temple was a live issue, as we see in Paul's writing (I Cor. 8.1–6) This anxiety reflected Jewish prohibitions. Similarly we see a reflection of Jewish concern about inter-faith marriage in Paul's more hopeful approach (I Cor. 7.12–16). But these were the inevitable problems when an ancient culture met a radical force. Paul's deeper struggle was about the place of Judaism in the purpose of God. He could write off his own national heritage as 'garbage' (Phil. 3.8) but also remember it with thanksgiving (Rom. 11.1). He could not believe that God had cast off Israel because Israel had cast out Jesus. He therefore hoped that the growth of Christian faith among the Gentiles would at some point in history persuade the people of the old covenant that they should trust in the new (Rom. 11.28–30). What is decisive is that the old law had no power to save, no strength to bring humanity into the presence of God, no world-wide application, no liberation of the soul.

For through faith you are all sons of God in union with Christ Jesus. Baptized into union with him, you have all put on Christ as a garment. There is no such thing as Jew and Greek, slave and freeman, male and female; for you are all one person in Christ Jesus. But if you thus belong to Christ, you are the 'issue' of Abraham, and so heirs by promise (Gal. 3.26–29).

Thus the Gospel broke out of the Jewish national life, away from exclusiveness, beyond patriotism, to make possible the new community where the old labels count for little and the welcome is open-armed and the greeting hands are scarred. That community was scattered as a tiny minority in the world of cults, philosophies, entrails, oracles, blood oaths, and power unlimited. It was international in the elementary sense for it quickly spread into Asia, Europe and north Africa. It was the beginning of a new prospect for humanity, true to the cross which had brought to a single point that love for all people which is the eternal nature of God.

CHAPTER FOUR

Courage and Compromise

The good news of Jesus Christ, taught by the apostles, transmitted by their lives, and experienced within the church fellowship, was a decisive break with the narrow boundaries of Israel. It has never been simple for the church to retain that vision. In every age there have been pressures to confine the church in national dress or to make the church a department of the state or to claim a favoured nation status in the eyes of God. In the early centuries it is probably wrong to speak of nationalism as the pressure. Yet there is something closely related – the allegiance to imperial authority which was set over the tribal loyalties of Europe. Both tribe and empire had claims on the life of citizens, just as nation states do today. Reaction to those claims may be a test of faith. Or it may be an opportunity for Christian witness. There is no simple correlation, and in this chapter I am concerned only to isolate a few instances of the interweaving of faith with nationalism as illustrations of the continuous story.

Civis Romanus sum was a claim that Paul was proud to use. This status 'was mine by birth' (Acts 22.28). But it was ambiguous indeed, for the state authority which should have provided protection from flogging also ensured the termination of his missionary vocation. In the mood of confident resignation Paul could write to Christians in Rome that the existing authorities are instituted by God, 'consequently anyone who rebels against authority is resisting a divine institution, and those who so resist have themselves to thank for the punishment they will receive' (Rom. 13.1–2). It was an attitude which could not endure. Indeed, it has always been difficult for interpreters of Paul to defend a case which makes no distinction between a righteous and a devilish ruler. From the days of the first Roman persecutions of the church, the Pauline teaching was undermined by events. Resistance to imperial claims became an act of courage and faith, not a sign of disobedience. So the writing of Paul has to be set alongside the vision of John where the imperial city and its aristocracy are seen as the object of God's anger with punishment in store. The enormous power of Rome was accustomed to show that religion belonged to the empire, as did law or armies. So the divine character of the emperor became a focus of imperial religion, a test of loyalty. Supreme Commander, final Judge and Divine Emperor – all formed consolidated power, and to this claim Christians with great courage had to say no.

So the early reaction of the church to the claims of hyper-nationalism was negative. It was not a rejection of the state or its right to govern, but of the claims made in its name which went beyond the requirements of good government into the area of the heart's devotion. Therefore the change of mind in the emperor Constantine in the year 312 removed one agony. His conversion led to the toleration of Christianity throughout the empire and ensured that no divine title would be claimed by the emperor. The rapid extension of Christian faith thereafter made a new challenge to Christians. As they were able to become officers of the state, soldiers of the state, advisers to the court and legislators, and as the properties of the church grew, so the life of the church became increasingly wedded to the life of the empire. This was reflected in the constitution of the church. Rome had to be the headquarters. There needed to be effective government. The priesthood required discipline and devotion. A hierarchy of orders was the natural ordering of a society. Special rights for the higher orders ensured a proper chain of command. All this was learnt, not from the wandering Galilean, but from the state apparatus of Rome.

But Rome also learnt from the church. The ruling class discovered that persons are equally persons whatever their order in society. The tottering statues of the pantheon were pushed further from the centre of life. The person of Jesus, so distant from the mainstream of Roman life, attracted many. Most of all, many people across the empire, in those days of increasing military weakness and outside threat, saw hope in the grace of God rather than the might of the emperor. At first sight it was as if a new empire was arising to replace the lost dynamic of the old. The crucial differences between them gave the church a higher standard than its own constitution, a wider range of thought than the imperial map, and a Lord whose crown and robe were the cruel jokes of authority. In its preaching, therefore, the Christian community was turning the world upside down. In its practice it was led towards constant compromise with the world as it is.

These early centuries of the church thus provide examples of two attitudes towards the state, which have been repeated throughout history. One is the rejection of state claims to worship, the ultimate sacralizing of the state. The other is the compromise of success when the church lives in the palace, and thereafter sits at ease with the powerful. That is too easy a contrast. Many Christians must have been caught between these positions and many lived out their devotion without any sense of a critical stance towards the state. These two attitudes, however, are important for us all, since they establish one model of Christian national concern.

The first is the point of judgment when Christians considered that state claims had to be resisted, even to death. The state had authority from God (John 19.11; Rom. 13.1) but it was not unlimited, and therefore any state might overstep the mark. The tendency to do so was endemic. In a world of autocrats and chiefs and generals who lived by the exercise of great power, there was always the possibility that they would demand types of obedience which religious people resisted. How should the judgment be made? Some of the Christian heroes of the early days took as their standard the things due to Caesar and the things due to God; they were confident that to offer sacrifices and to speak of a Lord belonged to worship of God alone. Looking back from a safe distance it appears to be an obvious and even inevitable decision. How else could they be faithful to the Lordship of Christ? But it is not often an obvious matter. It is more often a confused slide from the proper to the improper authority and command, at one moment an acceptable care for national security, for example, and the next an order to betray the political opposition. This complex movement has meant that Christians are rarely unanimous about the necessary time to say no to the state; this can well be regarded as a weakness in Christian witness.

The consequences of acceptance have been far more difficult. This became the standard pattern throughout the Roman empire and its successor regimes in Europe, and thus represents the status of Christianity most familiar to us. Under Constantine it was not one established religion but toleration for many which gave Christianity its freedom, but the personal conversion of the emperor made Christian faith respectable, advantageous and semi-official. Christian mission thereafter tended to aim at the conversion of chiefs in the expectation that popular assent would follow. Christianity would develop not by subversion but by edict, a strange reversal of the Gospel process. That generalization is not wholly true, for while the emissaries of Roman Christianity were usually approaching chiefs, there were always wandering preachers, particularly in the Celtic lands, who moved among peasants and foot soldiers as humble, hardy heralds of the Kingdom of God. Conversion from the top down, however, has been a difficult method of evangelism in every century, for it is bound to suggest that the faith is transmitted through political power. This sets up a tension between the experience of faith as officially supported and the Gospel story of the outsider who was rejected by both political and religious authority. But perhaps that very tension has been for the health of the state, which can look on Christian faith as a very critical ally, so that while the church itself may appear compromised its message always remains its judge.

The great empire gradually crumbled and the church power grew. The next phase shows us the two powers in close relationship, sometimes friends, sometimes in competition, sometimes hostile. If there were two cities, the earthly and the heavenly, then both had their rulers, and if God were the ruler of the heavenly city then the bishop of Rome was his regent. Twin pillars of civilization they appeared to many, as the security of the state was threatened. Supremacy moved from one to the other. As the empire began to disintegrate, so political power became distributed across Europe, and by the eighth century the Pope was able to recognize a Holy Roman Empire based outside Italy, north of the Alps. The church was catholic in outlook and intention, so looked for imperial power as the natural ally. The tribalism of Europe offered no defence against chaos (always the dark shadow in the medieval mind) and the charging hordes from the east were menacing. The birth of Islam was another sign of a power struggle. Faith and military might were again bound together in the great sweep across the Arabian deserts to the Mediterranean shores. So the alliance of the Pope with the Holy Roman Emperor was a defensive alliance for the life of Christian Europe. It became an offensive alliance with the Crusades. To us these seem the most extraordinary, misplaced, ill-conceived, muddled and corrupted Christian adventure, yet they called out supreme qualities in many people and may be seen by kindly historians as an attempt by the western church to give help to the eastern churches when threatened by Islam, a strange forerunner of inter-church aid. At this point the church was calling on the states for support to mount a series of military adventures over a period of nearly three centuries, and thus clearly established Christianity as a warlike religion against all the teaching of its founder.

This is typical of the compromises of power. When the church can effectively manipulate, persuade, direct and shape the policy of the state, then it has such power that it cannot renounce power, it is trapped by success and takes on the habits of the state. Yet this very compromise enables great demonstrations of faith. Social life can be touched by Christian values over a wide area, and this is part of the apostolic mission. It is, I believe, wholly sentimental to proclaim that only the church under persecution is doing the will of God. But it remains evident that the temptations of power are more pressing than the dangers of the minority oppressed by the regime, and the church through the ages has all too often pretended it is not so.

In the Middle Ages the tribe, the city and the empire were foci of loyalty. The rise of the modern nation state and the spirit of nationalism is frequently traced to the upheavals of Europe from the fourteenth to the seventeenth centuries. Yet that is a narrow view. It omits the development of centralized government in China and Japan, which were charting their own isolated way of social organization, and looks only at the western half of Europe. The change which is very significant for our purpose is that limited one from tribe/empire to nation state. The medieval synthesis provided both a very local loyalty and a broad concept of belonging, a horizon out of sight for many people but always there, at the edge of life. So a Saxon, for example, would know fully what it meant to be within a lord's territory and might only glimpse very occasionally the overlord, the emperor, the princes of the universal church. But the growth of national feeling meant that a clear, unified mass of people found an identity beyond that of the tribe and more localized than the empire. It has been a profound experience in every part of the world that has passed through this transition. In the modern world we have a host of visible examples. During the period of growth in national identity strongman government emerges as one of the dynamic factors – Bismark in Germany, Banda in Malawi, Kaunda in Zambia, Lee Kwan Yu in Singapore are examples. Even so, the process is fragile and the new identity is liable to assault by the older tribalism as we can note from the Wars of the Roses in England to the Biafran war in Nigeria.

How has Christianity viewed this powerful development in human history? Generally, with an approval tinged with fear. During the Reformation period the hope of many leading Christians in Europe was that the local princes would continue to exercise authority in religious matters but now in favour of Reformation church views. So in England the growing independence of English authority over against Rome was a national rejection of the supra-national medieval synthesis (always a weak influence in the off-shore island). There was to be a truly English church to parallel the English state. The beginnings of that movement are seen in the life of John Wycliffe who

25

influenced many people beyond England, especially John Hus in Bohemia. These two also illustrate the power of language. They led the way out of the dominance of Latin – universal but learned – into the era of the vernacular. Luther gives that movement its crown, and the amazement to us is that it then took a further four centuries for the Roman church to appreciate the immense value of worshipping God in the language we use at home.

The blessing of the church for the process of nationalism has been most marked in this century. Many Christian leaders have recognized in the ending of old empires and the emergence of new nations a movement to lift the human spirit, encourage human talent, and provide that responsibility of choice and that freedom which can be seen as part of God's purpose for us all. I have heard African preachers, particularly in the 1960s, speaking powerfully of the liberation struggle and the establishment of the new state as the exodus, God's deliverance, and the promised land. Here I find an echo of the seventeenth-century struggle in England when the overthrow of the monarchy was welcomed by a great many preachers in similar terms. The Pharaoh had been brought to trial and God's people were now responsible for fashioning their own life. It is a common enough interpretation. Salvation history is our history. We are God's people and our oppressors are the enemies of the Lord of Hosts. It is also a highly dangerous interpretation, but that is more evident to the onlooker than to the protagonist. It is a point to which we shall return.

This long period in which the nation states of Europe were developing was also the time of confused, inspiring dynamic which we know as the Reformation. No doubt the two processes were related, but not mutually dependent. It is common today to express much criticism of Luther and Calvin regarding their expression of church-state relations, but I believe we become more understanding if we see from what they were emerging rather than compare them with the more liberal or secular philosophy of today. Behind the Reformers was that synthesis of princes, lords and bishops as allies, wedded by common interest and often by common corruption. Beyond them was chaos and the likelihood of prolonged civil war. Luther developed close links with those princes who were sympathetic and asked their permission and authority for the process of regularizing reformed worship in their territory. It was not an Erastian solution, for Luther at no point urged princes, even the most pious, to exercise control in church affairs, but it was paving the way for the 'concordat church' or established religion which became characteristic of nations with Lutheran majorities. Luther was ready to give advice to princes. He is reputed to have said, 'One should rebuke secular rulers if they allow the goods of their poor subjects to be drained off and ruined by usury and bad government. But it is not proper for a preacher to prescribe measures and say at what price bread, meat, etc. should be sold and valued' (*Letters of Spiritual Counsel*, SCM Press 1955; Library of Christian Classics, a quotation from the Table Talk of 1540). This was an essentially conservative attitude to state authority, and when Luther approved of the princes' military opposition to the Peasants' Revolt of 1524 he was affirming the God-given power of the state. Even so it is surprising that he went so far in that direction. To publish a pamphlet 'Against the Murderous and Thieving Hordes of Peasants' was perhaps a sign of the great reluctance with which Luther made a break with the past, and his need of princely protection. It is this content with the status quo and this 'concordat church' which has made it hard for the historic Lutheran churches to take up radical positions against authority, an agony for many German Christians in the Nazi period. Only in Southern Africa, particularly in Namibia, have Lutherans as a body revealed a readiness to take the path of political risk. But for all this acceptance of the state, Luther brings so many flashes of insight to public affairs that we all remain in his debt. One example on our theme is a letter he wrote to Prince Joachim of Brandenburg in 1532 when the Prince had been selected to lead the Saxon army against the Turks. Luther advised on the attitude of those engaged in such a war.

> I beg that those on our side may not place their reliance on the Turk's being altogether wrong and God's enemy while we are innocent and righteous in comparison with the Turk, for such presumption is also vain. Rather it is necessary to fight with fear of God and reliance on his grace alone. We too are unrighteous in God's sight. Some on our side have shed much innocent blood, have despised and persecuted God's word and have been disobedient and so we cannot take our stand on our merits, no matter how righteous or unrighteous the Turks and we may be (*Letters*, p. 331).

There we recognize the evangelical spirit which dominated the thinking of Luther in all his best work. It was not Luther who promulgated the phrase *cuius regio, eius religio* (the ruler decides the religion of his country) for that came at the Peace of Augsburg, nine years after Luther's death; but the trend is faithful to his life – care for stability and order in a dangerous world.

Calvin moved further. His reform, although based so firmly on the scripture, pushed the authority of the church to a limit which can only be compared with the Roman Catholic ascendancy in Latin America in the eighteenth and nineteenth centuries. He started from the biblical position that state authority had been ordained by God and even wicked rulers held office through that divine ordinance. It was not for individuals to rebel against that authority.

> If we are cruelly tormented by a savage, if we are rapaciously pillaged by an avaricious or luxurious, if we are neglected by a sluggish, if, in short, we are persecuted for righteousness' sake by an impious and sacrilegious prince, let us first call up the remembrance of our faults, which doubtless the Lord is chastising by such scourges. In this way humility will curb our impatience. And let us reflect that it belongs not to us to cure these evils, that all that remains for us is to implore the help of the Lord, in whose hands are the hearts of kings and inclinations of kingdoms (*Institutes of the Christian Religion*, IV. 20, 29, trans. Beveridge, James Clarke 1953).

There could be no more passionate defence of the hands-off policy. Yet Calvin could not remain there. He goes on, in the *Institutes*, to offer two balancing demands. The first is that the properly constituted estates of the realm, which he calls the 'three orders', do have a duty to oppose a wicked ruler. Indeed, if they fail to do so 'they fraudulently betray the liberty of the people, while knowing that, by the ordinance of God, they are its appointed guardians'. The second opposition arises when the obedience demanded by the state conflicts with obedience to God. 'We are subject to the men who rule over us, but subject only in the Lord.' So if they command anything against the will and word of God, 'let us not pay the least regard to it, nor be moved by all the dignity which they possess as magistrates'. There is a deep mis-match here, for the latter instruction provides precisely the ground for personal disobedience to the state which humble patience forbids. Calvin in his life and work accepted this power of Christian conscience to criticize, condemn, instruct, and even dominate the state. For he came to regard the church as the receptor of God's truth and therefore as superior to every other kind of authority. He felt at home in instructing the Genevan state council on their duty to pass particular laws and in imposing church laws which welded together a harsh and pious regime which left little room for the dissenter. We can perhaps sense a little of that marriage of state and church in the stern, cruel regime of the South African government as it operates with the Dutch Reformed Church in that country. When considering different varieties of government Calvin expressed a preference for a republic.

Monarchy, he wrote, is prone to tyranny, even though it has a divine sanction.

> It is safer and more tolerable when many bear rule, that they may thus mutually assist, instruct and admonish each other, and should any one be disposed to go too far, the others are censors and masters to curb his excess (*Institutes*, IV, 20.8).

So Calvin developed a position, both in his own person and in his writing, that goes well beyond the New Testament vision and places the church in a status of great influence as the teacher of the state, for the sake of progress to a holy society. We see the effects of this in many parts of the world, from Scotland to New England and to those island communities in the South Pacific so powerfully touched by Calvinist missionaries in the nineteenth century.

But that century also saw the great extension of national powers. In Europe we see that particularly in Germany and Italy as each collection of princely states was welded into a clearly defined nation. In Germany the Protestant churches had been established by the individual states and that pattern remained after unification under Prussian leadership. The style of establishment varied but generally provided that all citizens were deemed to be members of the official church unless they deliberately opted out, so the church owed a duty to all and in return the state collected a church tax and supported the charitable work of the church and, frequently, its ministry. It is a pattern which remains in the Federal Republic despite the radically altered social mix of the population. Today it presents a puzzle to church leaders who find this cushion of establishment a doubtful advantage for educating the church in the realities of mission.

In Italy the unification of the state took place beside the ancient claims of the papacy. I believe it is right to note the influence of the one on the other. Political claims by the pope in what were called the Papal States of central Italy had long been defended by the church, and that defence was backed by troops sent by Catholic nations, particularly by France. So when the uprisings took place which led to unification, those Papal States remained as an island of ancient autocracy. Then, in 1870, France had to face the military onslaught of Prussia and withdrew all troops from Italy to defend the homeland. The pope had no other forces. The national movement swept forward to the gates of the Vatican and firmly established the king and government of the new Italy in the heart of Rome. The date is significant. For that was the year of the Vatican Council when papal power in the church was elevated and enforced. Having lost all temporal or political rule, the

Vatican pushed through the council those declarations of papal infallibility which have impeded any reconciliation of the churches ever since. It was, at least in part, a defensive reaction to the loss of power. Another aspect of this was the steady Italian dominance of the Curia despite the international character of the Roman Catholic church. In the nineteenth century this did not create any crisis, but it helped to reinforce the concept of the Italian church as the centre and all else as peripheral. The growth of Italian nationalism did not diminish this reality, and it is only in recent years that any major change has occurred. Did the church welcome the nationalist movement? Not when it threatened papal powers. But once the new state was established the Vatican soon came to terms with it, co-operated and rested reasonably content with its own tiny enclave of independence.

A very different variety of nationalism developed across the Atlantic where the enormous resources of a continent were exploited by the rapidly growing power of the United States. Two distinctive factors marked it off from European nation-building. The first was the possibility of expansion in a largely empty land mass, so there was no drive for overseas colonies and no sense of defensive boundaries. This made a large measure of freedom possible. The second was the room for diversity. From the original States the concept of state rights remained strong, while at first federal government was weak; people could move to a state where their opportunity was greatest. The influx of many ethnic groups caused friction but also generated great energy. It also affirmed the plural religious philosophy which caused the brave writers of the constitution to ensure separation of church and state. Unlike the western European experience and the Orthodoxy of eastern Europe, there was no drive in America to retain a mono-credal state, a monopoly church or a monolithic establishment. Yet there is no evidence that Christian influence was diminished. In fact it grew, but into peculiar shapes. For the very freedom of individual and ethnic development encouraged the variety of sects to astonish the world, and the theologians to pursue many strange ideas and the hot gospel evangelists to increase their decibels. How could so diverse a Christian presence react to the growing national power of the United States? It could only welcome and bless and participate. Where a thousand sects opened their doors, the hunting of heretics became a futile task. Where wealth was generated through the enterprise of business corporations, the church could operate with equal dash and efficiency and become rich too. Until the middle of this century there does not seem to have been major Christian critique of the national spirit or the national policy. Since then, issues like Vietnam, nuclear weapons, Nicaragua and poverty have shaken loose the mutual admiration of church and state.

In these small snapshots of such relationships across Christian history we can note all the major trends which are still visible today:

1. The powerless minority oppressed by the state; the faithful few. Most vivid for our generation is the Chinese church during the cultural revolution, but there is a line of descent from apostolic times.

2. The church of size and weight in conflict with a state regime. From Thomas Becket to Father Popieluszko and Archbishop Romero, Bonhoeffer and Janani Luwum.

3. The church and state in uneasy partnership or rivalry, acknowledging each other but keeping a keen eye for an advantage. We have a close example of that in the Republic of Ireland during the Garret Fitzgerald years.

4. The church and state remaining distinct yet in very close alliance, as in the Spain of Franco and the Argentine during the military junta.

5. The theocracy in which the church, professing its search for the Kingdom here on earth, holds political power. Some Orthodox churches have come close to this, and Archbishop Makarios in Cyprus provides a symbol of it.

6. Caesaropapism (and I shudder to write such a word) when the state authority effectively controls the life of the church. There are no full-blown examples today but many observers see features of it in the hard-line socialist regimes of eastern Europe.

7. Making the state sacred so that worship and patriotism are indistinguishable. This was the Japanese pattern for generations, now formally disentangled. It needs a strong hierarchical society to make this possible.

8. The secular state, taking an independent view of all churches and religions, with Christians at a distance from political influence except by individual participation. This is today's popular trend, from USA to Australia.

There are, of course, no absolute boundaries of these positions and one may shade into another. Neither is there any obvious order of preference. We cannot easily form an objective judgment when Christians have struggled to express their faith under so many conditions in the great complexity of human societies. The only position in this list which is untenable by Christians is (7), and even that coloured the feudal hierarchy and the divine right of kings as in the

France of Louis XIV; no Christian theologian would have proclaimed divinization of the state, but many Christians slipped into that attitude.

Most significant for us is the fact that so few Christians, in any of these situations, have retained a critical stance towards nationhood itself. While many have opposed conscientiously the particular style of national government or policy, there have been only isolated cases of Christians who, while being part of the nation, have yet seen far greater realities than the nation which commands our duty. In this short list we honour Francisco de Vitoria, a Dominican who taught theology at the University of Salamanca in northern Spain in the first half of the sixteenth century. He spoke about the community of nations as broad as the human race, and urged that no national policy should be pursued if it caused greater harm to that world community. He was followed by Hugo Grotius, a Dutch Protestant and by William Penn whose vision of European federation offers remarkable glimpses of the future. We owe much to the Quakers for continual reminders that the nation itself is not a self-contained unit and needs to be balanced at all times by a wider love and a larger hope.

We accept the world. That's how it is. The nation is all we've got. All of us have this pragmatic sense of living in a fixed order of human society which stretches forward for eternity, and therefore making our peace with it. That is the essential compromise for any orderly corporate life. But it leaves open the question whether an increase in the power, wealth, extent and glory of the nation can be a Christian objective in our small world. And can the church – particularly in the Protestant tradition – remain content to order its life in national boundaries?

CHAPTER FIVE

British Ambiguities

It was in the early 70s that I first became aware of the phrase 'the four nations' as applied to these islands. There may have been many earlier uses of the words but they reached me through the British Council of Churches and particularly through that visionary leader Harry Morton. In church circles we have used the phrase increasingly since then. It has been an endeavour to recognize the distinctiveness of the units which make up the British Isles and therefore a welcome correction to the English assumption that England and Britain are the same thing. But it remains an elusive phrase, easily misunderstood, and not entirely satisfactory. Is the United Kingdom one nation, or three, or four?

This is not an abstract discussion for it is part of the Irish agony and Irish dream, where the concept of nationalism is so confused and so intertwined with religion. As we have looked at tribalism in the background of national life elsewhere, we can do so also in these islands, thinking of the many distinctive tribes that formed the population in Roman times. As the Roman power entered through the south east and from there spread to the mountains of the north and the west, so there was a periphery, an area where Roman law was unknown and different languages never absorbed Latin words. When Normans invaded and settled the same process happened, so that two periods of cohesion formed some sense of unity in England. Ireland remained beyond these colonizers and so missed their influence and also their enforcement of order. The church in Ireland was the unifying force, and during the great centuries brought life and light to the areas we know as Scotland and northern England and Wales. So when the English colonizers, in wayward, arrogant and adventurous moods, brought their private troops into Ireland there was a confrontation of cultures and faiths as well as lords. We have to confess the great ills caused by English occupation in Ireland. It was

33

never thoroughly accomplished but half achieved. It alienated land to absentee landlords and projected an image of the Irish as a servant people. From Elizabeth I onwards, the English court was able to brush off the claims of the Irish as the noise of a rabble. So until the nineteenth century the Protestant way of faith was for the gentry and the Roman Catholic or Celtic way was for below stairs – a generalization which is nurtured in mythology. Certainly the disadvantages for Catholics were cruel.

The settlement of Scots in the north added another layer of dominance. It was, in a sense, a Protestant colony or plantation in which once again the Irish Catholics were the labour force. So the long story of Irish nationalism is a tale of tears – too close to England to be alone, never close to England in culture; subjugated by Protestants who were supposed to believe in liberty; looking back to a golden age of faith; sensing the values of the heart but driven to expediency by poverty; knowing an identity yet never expressing it to the full. When I visit churches in Ireland there is often an opportunity to meet a group of elders, of grand Presbyterian solidity in a solid Ulster town, and I have sometimes dropped into the conversation the question, 'Are you Irish?' and that is sufficient stimulus for the night. 'Of course we are British, but, yes, we are Irish too.' 'No, I'm not Irish at all,' says another, speaking in what I would call an Irish accent. There, in the north, the nationalisms are confused and the two identities sit side by side in a town and in a personality. The churches have, in the main, sought to understand and embrace the strange mixture of loyalties. All the principal denominations have one basis for the whole island, one synod, one conference. For church affairs the border is not allowed to be a barrier. Church leaders spend time in listening to other points of view and working with others. Yet the overall impression that British people have is that Irish Christians are wholly trapped within the two distinct nationalisms. It is partly true. However understanding and tolerant a pastor or a priest may be, he is under pressure from the more extreme members of the congregation to wave the national flag. To fail can then be cited as disloyalty.

All the churches in Ireland have been at one in denouncing the violence of the terrorists, though occasionally the voice has been muted. The denunciation is based on Christian respect for human life and for the constitutional process by which we can live together, recognizing one another's rights. Yet the nationalist who turns to violence can point to the achievements of violence in many parts of the world. It was ironic to hear the Pope, during his Irish visit, speak so plainly against violence – murder is murder and violence never achieves anything. Yet modern Poland as a nation only exists because of prolonged, courageous violence by nationalists in the past. One meaning of the theological phrase 'a fallen world' is that violence often does achieve something. The thrones and authorities frequently listen to no other voice. What the Irish churches are trying to say is therefore more complex. When constitutional and peaceful ways to change are open, when every citizen has an equal right to vote, then there is no excuse for turning to murder. It is a rejection of our modern social compact and a return to the jungle. Of course the constitutionalists have also to show that ways to change are open. If the underlying argument is 'accept the constitutional and peaceful way of life, but recognize that there will *never* be a government of your sort', then confidence in the ballot box drains away like water in the bath, leaving only froth and bubbles. Every minority in a democratic state hopes that by persuasion or alliances or influx it will become a majority, or, alternatively is so aware of equal rights, opportunities and freedoms that exclusion from power is no hardship. Different groups in Northern Ireland would hope in each half of that sentence.

Is there an Irish nation? Without doubt. It exists through the length of its history, its culture, its ability to govern, its sense of roots in a clearly defined area and in its relationship with nation states across the world. Nothing reveals the quality of nationhood in Eire better than its contribution to United Nations' peacekeeping forces and its giving to international aid and development. Here it is in the forefront of the nations, setting a standard for Europe. Is Northern Ireland a nation? My answer is no. It is part of two nations, for it contains two loyalties, two roots, two hopes and, in some city areas, two flags. This is the price paid by the Unionist population for the fact of partition. Where two nationalisms exist in a small area (Cyprus, Sri Lanka), partition is peaceful if the actual communities can occupy one side of the line and remain content in that boundary. Where they are mixed, as in Northern Ireland, I believe that the public institutions have in some way to acknowledge the two nationalisms side by side. If there should be a single state for the whole island, then it too would have to acknowledge the two entities in its life.

For the churches there will continue to be a delicate but vital task in acknowledging both natural aspirations but refusing to be locked into either box. The Roman Catholic church in Ireland does not exist for Irish nationalism. The Presbyterian church does not live for unionism. Both live and work and pray for something much greater, a vision beyond the boundaries. That is the calling. The harder the context the greater the obedience.

In Scotland and Wales the story of nationalism has been a little less complex and, in recent times, less violent. But it is still not a simple matter. The Scots were for a long period divided into highlanders and lowlanders with little in common, and it was among the lowlanders that a cosmopolitan society grew in the eighteenth century and an industrial society with all its multiform trading links in the nineteenth century. The great unifying force has always been the weight of English majorities to the south, rather than a single history. Many factors contribute to the present sense of being one Scottish people. The union of the two crowns, and particularly the Scottish affinities of royalty over the last 150 years; the mobility of Scots, often driven by depression or eviction, and thus the growth of romantic memory; the great commercial and industrial enterprises which have sought Scottish skills; the quality of the public education system; and the Church of Scotland as, in some ways, a public voice for the people. Scottish nationalism rests on the sense of being a distinctive people and, in recent years, only a small minority has wished to carry over that sense into a separate nation state. The economic, social and cultural links across the border are now so many and so strong that few people can envisage an independent Scotland. Yet there is a sense of nationhood, reinforced by the industrial decline and the conviction that all good things are concentrated in the south of England, leaving Scotland at the extremity of British life. The present British government has shown great insensitivity to this, with the result that many Scots now feel they are ruled by an alien government, speaking in a foreign accent, lacking any comprehension of their needs.

Such an impasse is likely to be reflected in Christian witness. A distinctive feature of church relationships within Scotland has been the extraordinary Presbyterian emotionalism whenever an episcopal or oversight ministry has been suggested as one element in a unified church order. Perhaps this reaction has been engineered by the press rather than the theologians, and portrayed in terms of betrayal not because such ministry is against the will of God but rather because it is English. The folk memory of the imposition of English government and English church may still underlie the debate. Another aspect is clearly the issue of size. For the Episcopal church to move the Church of Scotland in the direction of episcopacy – or for the Congregationalists to move it towards independency – is rather like the corner grocery shop seeking to change the policies of Marks and Spencer before a merger. The large body feels no impetus to change. This – if it is true – is a tragedy, for it means that size and not truth, numbers and not spiritual vitality call the tune. And if that is so, then the church has surrendered to politics. Another result, which we will look at later, is the greater reluctance of Scottish churches to throw their weight into British institutions or movements, seeing priority 'at home'.

Rather similar reflection arises when we look at the Welsh scene. The same sense of the periphery is there, the same minority facing an English majority, the same loss of that dynamism which came from industrial importance. But there are two major differences. First must come the Welsh language as the single most significant strand in Welsh nationalism. It is an irreplaceable treasure for those brought up within it, an identity with which no Englishman can argue, a defence tougher than castle walls. The fact that the language does not define the nation and now is spoken by a minority within Wales is recognized as a weakness in Welsh nationalism. Yet many in Wales who do not speak Welsh would value the language as a sign of distinctiveness and hope that their children might learn it in school. The language has had a profound effect on church life, both stimulating Welsh scholarship, preaching and hymnody and defining Welsh language congregations and denominations. Thus the Presbyterian Church of Wales has lived in two sections, one for each language; the United Reformed Church speaks English; the Union of Welsh Independents speaks Welsh; and the Anglican Church in Wales endeavours to be bilingual. There is a cost. It is both a financial burden for translation and interpretation, and a high risk of losing the fullness of fellowship. But we are not given treasures cost-free.

The second very distinctive element is the lack of one dominant tradition of churchmanship. Catholicism in Ireland, Presbyterianism in Scotland and Anglicanism in England each came to a point of dominance which, until the modern period, could hardly be questioned. But Wales has had a more open, plural Christian experience. It has, over the last two centuries, been predominantly non-conformist, that is, non-Anglican. No single strand of reformation churchmanship has carried the day. The innate risks of division through the lack of any common church authority, the emergence of powerful evangelists each with a following, and the independence of small isolated communities, all contributed to the diversity. This means that with no overwhelming denomination, the churches meet on a basis of equality. A question which we might wish to put is whether this factor has helped or hindered the effective public witness on social issues. I believe it has helped the Welsh churches to move into the Covenant for Unity.

In the past there have been disparaging comments on 'the Celtic fringe'. It has been an English way of dismissing the validity of experience in Ireland, Scotland and Wales. In social and in church life the phrase is wholly misleading, for it suggests that somehow the English experience is more central for British life. But the periphery is often the place of growth. The Celtic energy has infused the static establishment style of central English habits just as the Celtic faith was light from the horizon. The drawbacks have been just that – the drawing back of a culture to the past and a supposed golden age. In Scotland and Wales such a backward look has generated much sentimentality, but in Ireland it has ensured the continued fighting of ancient battles, the division of community and church, and the sorrows of sectarianism. The greatest test for all who today affect public morale is whether they hold up realistic hope for the post-Celtic communities and work towards its achievement.

How hard it is for an Englishman even to touch the realities and aspirations which form nationalism in Ireland, Scotland and Wales, but hard also to understand what English nationalism is. There is not an easily identifiable character, nor a single cultural expression. The closest we come to it is the crown and the court, the sitting of Parliament, the style of BBC English, the performance of Shakespeare, the Oxbridge education, the Anglican gentleness, the white cliffs of Dover – but then we realize that a hundred other quite different experiences are just as crucial. Nationalism in Durham or Kings Lynn or Exeter does not focus on London. There is a sense of an English fringe as well as a Celtic one. Regionalism has been with us since the tribal days of the East, West and South Saxons, and has never been wholly lost in the cosmopolitan life of our cities. During the last generation we saw a major influx of new elements into the English social mix. To be English today may mean that you have a Norman or Norse ancestry but equally that you look to Barbados, Jamaica, Bangladesh or Uganda as the place where your family began. This is the greatest permanent change in our population, significant for governments, churches and all social institutions as we seek to provide a just framework of life for all our people.

So there are many identities. But is there an English nation? I find it a strain on words, something that is forced and not arising from experience. National action for me does not mean English people on their own; national policy is not English – it is British. That unity under one government and crown means more than any artificial English separate identity. Yet this is just another version of superiority in which we assume that our English numbers will inevitably carry the day and decide the future. The ambiguity is obvious and lives in us all. This is why English people need constant education in the meaning of nationalism as it touches people in the other parts of the United Kingdom. Repeated, gratuitous insensitivity over the centuries has been the soil in which the seeds of resentment have been kept alive. The appointment by the Prime Minister of a Secretary of State for Wales who is an English MP living in England is one recent indication of our general inability to see through the eyes of the minority.

The ambiguity of four nations/one nation is evident in much of our international life. At the United Nations or the Commonwealth Secretariat there is acceptance that one government is the key to being a nation. The United Kingdom is therefore one nation. When matters are less serious, as at the Commonwealth Games, we allow the four nations a place. The Vatican, in its own idiosyncratic way, deals with three elements, Scotland, Ireland and England plus Wales. To stress the four nations can be regarded as pandering to an ancient framework of life which pleases sentimentality but has nothing to say to the great institutions and power bases of today. To stress the one nation can equally be seen as a blatant disregard of identities which are precious, and a further downgrading of the periphery. I do not believe that in this case compromise is a weakness; it is the way to realistic life. The churches in Britain need to contribute to that compromise by showing that the national boundaries are important yet never all-important, that the different accents of faith are valued but never become a Babel of misunderstanding, and that the exchange of persons is as easy and frequent in church life as it is in the universities or the major industries. The political compromise will involve devolution of some sort; not federalism in which separate states cede some power to the centre. In church life the national denominations are currently so fixed in their boundaries that federalism may be required.

The more we use the phrase 'the four nations' – and I do not believe it can now be dropped – the more the churches are committed to cultural and political expressions of nationalism. We need also to think of one United Kingdom. Churches will acknowledge boundaries and transcend them. So the ambiguity is not loss but realism; it is recognizing the character of the people of these islands with diverse identities. There is one nation, and that a middle-ranking one in the whole community of nations, but it is made up of communities which are distinctive. The most difficult application of this two-sided coin is in Ireland. To speak of four nations without conceding the aims of Irish nationalism is very difficult. I do not think that church leaders in

Britain have yet come fully to terms with this, nor have they reflected fully on what was involved in the 1920s in the acceptance of minority pressure in the island to effect a partition. I do not feel that a plea for 'three and a half nations' has any validity.

The Christian Gospel has had a powerful influence in shaping British life as our cities and towns and villages bear witness, and as our great national institutions reveal. It has been seen as an ally of the national spirit through most of our history. Faith, made visible in churchmanship, has been built into the fabric of our society. It is now crumbling. The fabric is worn and frayed. How do we stand as churches in this world of national security, of polychrome populations, of materialist ambitions? Can there be a national church any longer?

CHAPTER SIX

The National Church

There is no more powerful symbol of the nation state and the national church than a coronation. It is the most public witness possible that earthly rule and heavenly rule are related, even married. It goes back a long way in European history, as we noted in Chapter Four. Here we look first at a variety of national churches, their advantages and drawbacks, and question whether the current British solution is sufficient for our modern society.

A national church means that there is one officially recognized and represented church which has a place in the socio-political world, however many other churches may exist. I met this situation as a young minister in the islands of Polynesia and Micronesia – an unlikely context. There we were in a region where the first great missionary impact had come from England in the shape of dissenters, independents or what we now call Congregationalists, through the enterprise of the London Missionary Society. There had been a great effort to convert local chiefs, and where this was successful the tribe had followed them into the embrace of British nonconformity. So in the mid-twentieth century there remained a majority church, professing a Reformed faith, which occupied the honoured place on all civic occasions, which could whisper in the chief's ear, which could mobilize resistance to colonial government, and which could look down, with a rather superior smile, at the Roman Catholics, the Adventists and other more recent arrivals. There was one small island which passed a local law that everyone on the island must belong to the one church. The rule was tested by the Roman Catholic bishop, who was chased down the beach by Protestant vigilantes and had to go off to his ship in some disarray. That was the end of the rule. For the might of the United Nations was called on to declare that basic freedom of worship was being denied.

That experience of an unofficial national church has made me more aware of the variety of privileges given to the church in many parts of the world. The Lutheran churches of western Europe have, in many cases, a close official link which arises from the royal or princely acceptance of the Reformation in the sixteenth and seventeenth centuries. In the Federal Republic of Germany this means that every citizen is deemed to be subject to the pastoral care of the one Lutheran/Evangelical church unless there is individual opting out. The state therefore acknowledges the church's great social responsibility by collecting a church tax. The concept of *Volk Kirche* probably stems from nineteenth century romanticism, but is now very widely used as a sign of the service which the church is committed to give to the whole community. It suggests a unity which disappeared at least a generation ago. In Scandinavia, the Lutheran establishment is more clearly defined, with the state having a major rôle in the constitution of the church and the appointment and payment of clergy. This is seen, formally, as payment for conducting statutory services, but in effect it is the provision of a civil servant's salary. In eastern Europe the national church is often Orthodox and where the church has freedom, as in Greece, it occupies a central place in community life and in the intellectual life of the nation. Its relationship with the government varies with the political trend, and radicalism in government casts a chill over the clerical establishment. In Romania the Orthodox church, even under a hard-line socialist regime, has retained a sufficiently establishment ethos to look smugly at the disadvantages of minority denominations. The Orthodox in eastern Europe have generally resisted, with a variety of tools, the influx of any other varieties of religious discipline, believing that nation and church belong together in unity. For this reason there is vocal concern about 'proselytism' whenever evangelism is discussed. The millennium of the Russian Orthodox Church in 1988 provides an opportunity for its leaders both to declare all that the church has meant to the nation and to enlarge the ground of faith in the tough modern context. It could also be an occasion for acts of mutual acceptance with Baptist groups, and that would be an imaginative use of the protective limelight during the celebrations.

We recognize Roman Catholicism in several countries occupying the position of a national church, not so much by law as by numbers, weight, history and high public profile. It is hard for one who comes from a minority English church background to appreciate the meaning of Catholic omnipresence in Italy or Spain or Ireland. At one moment it seems lethargic, as though the stones of a thousand cathedrals are pressing down the spirit of enterprise and the call to pilgrimage, with the tombs of the saints as the most sparkling element in a black-robed life. But yet the vigour of faith breaks through. These vast clerical pyramids suddenly reveal an opening and salty theology or psychological wisdom bursts out. The impact on public life is dubious. There is a blessing of conservative politics which, in the past, provided a moral cushion for General Franco and is still a strange consequence of the revolutionary Christian message. This combined weight of church and state on the conservative side of the scales is one reason why Communism has developed as a counterpoise, for only the most persistent radical forces are seen in Italy, for example, as able to mount an effective challenge. The public policy of the church is most frequently made known on moral issues. The Irish referendum on divorce revealed the strength of clergy advice against a mildly reformist government, and this carried the day. It provides us with an example of the power of a great majority church which effectively ensures that people of other persuasions must abide by the moral judgments of the church. The same process has occurred in Protestant countries. We need to consider this pressure to conform as we evaluate national churches.

So we turn to Britain and the two national churches which so deeply affect the entire religious scene in England and Scotland. Although they have little in common from the viewpoint of ecclesiology, their stance as national churches creates similarities of style. Both accept a moral responsibility for providing Christian ministry in every part of the nation. To be national means that every village should see the church in its midst. To be established means that there is some legal weight behind this responsibility; it is not just a self-generated claim. The two forms of establishment reflect the depth of Reformation theology which inspired the leaders of church and state in Scotland and England, and the measure of freedom which the church had in that period to adapt its form to its theology. In Scotland the focus of Reformation was more radical than in England, since the Genevan model carried greatest conviction, and was proclaimed by John Knox in the key years between 1550 and 1560. In England the pre-emptive strike by the throne meant that in the critical period between 1520 and 1550 there was a variety of Reformation voices, no broad consensus and only divided churchmen to oppose the autocratic intentions of Henry VIII. He was able to break with Rome and make himself the equivalent of the pope in England, 'supreme head on earth of the English Church'. The muddled origins of the Church of England as a body separated from Rome ensured that in its faith and theology it would be a church holding a Reformed interpretation of Catholic faith, while in government it would be solidly nationalist, crown and mitre wedded. The development from those beginnings has been slow and pragmatic. Space, tolerance, equality and fellowship with other churches was slow in coming. The rights of the crown were partially transferred to parliament and then, by very careful steps, partially transferred to the church's own synod. Thus, while in Scotland Presbyterianism was recognized as the national church of the Scots and the doctrinal assurance made it impossible to accede to royal or parliamentary control, the English settlement has led us to a national church over which parliament and crown retain residuary powers.

Across Europe we thus see the growth of national churches from all the major Christian traditions – Orthodox, Roman Catholic, Lutheran, Calvinist, Anglican. They are a mark of success. When the faith has been accepted by large majorities then the organized church becomes powerful, its influence spreads into every dimension of life, and those who are authorities in the church are allied to the authorities in politics and intellectual life. Some of these large churches are still established by law. That raises very serious questions. But the very fact of national churches at once poses the issue whether the Christian church can ever belong to the nation. By what right do we take national boundaries to be church boundaries? Has not the nation state assumed too large a position in our thought and practice? How can the salvation of Christ be demonstrated if his body is divided into national as well as denominational elements? There is thus a strong argument for lessening the national and increasing the international element in Christian life. But I now turn to the question of legal establishment, at which point we see nationalism carried to one of its logical conclusions.

I approach this question from the background of the Reformed church in which I serve and the ecumenical journey in which I have been a participant. Two valuable recent treatments of the subject are contained in *The British: Their Identity and Their Religion* by Daniel Jenkins (1975) and *Church and Nation in a Secular Age* by John Habgood (1983). The first of these considers the religious groupings in relation to the sociology of the British people, finding that the variety is entirely appropriate, with each being called to offer particular talents. Thus the Free Church should be pressing for freedom in thought and life, while the established church should minister to the agencies of national power. The correlation of churchmanship and culture is surely a very important aspect of our experience of Christ. My main question is whether that correlation should be determinative. John Habgood quotes Daniel Jenkins with approval as he offers his own defence of the establishment of the Church of England. It is good to have this view from the Archbishop who has given wholehearted service to the ecumenical movement and who reflects on the life of his own church from very great experience of national concerns. But looking from the outside, I find his argument not entirely convincing.

He has cited four main criticisms of the legal establishment and sought to answer them. The first is that establishment is a delusion because it obscures the true and desperate state of religion in England; his response is that there is no delusion in the sense of responsibility given to the church to care for everyone. John Habgood fears that a departure from the establishment would quickly lead towards a denominationalism in which a circle would be drawn around those who are members. I would press the further question whether the delusion is actually hindering the radical missionary task and calling by its assumption of a very broad Christian base. Responsibility for that task is shared by all the churches, and we have not seen that establishment helps the Church of England to lead us all in working for the evangelization of the nation together.

The second argument is about privilege. The critic may point towards the high seats occupied by the Anglican hierarchy. Dr Habgood responds by suggesting that such few privileges as remain are to be used as the entry point into the power structures of our land. He reacts warmly to Daniel Jenkins' suggestion that the Church of England has a particular duty, on behalf of all, to minister to people in power. But I fear that the Church of England cannot have it both ways. If God's bias to the poor is a scriptural reality, and if the Christian faith means so great an ethical revolution that the forgotten people of society are those who best know God's love, then to allocate to any church the sphere of ministry to the powerful is very dangerous. It is likely to cloud the vision. Though I honour those Anglicans who retain a radical understanding of the forces shaping human life, I often wonder if their position in society does not tear them apart.

The third argument is about spiritual freedom. John Habgood believes that parliamentary control today is residual in extent and generally beneficial, and that it does not hinder freedom of expression. I do not think he has fully answered the theological point at issue, which is the proper ordering of the company of people who form the body of Christ. How can that company cede to another authority any key decision about its worship, its leaders, its theology or its forms of ministry? We well understand how the position has arisen historically. But that members of the Church of England should submit to the system, Erastian in essence, is surprising and alarming. That there is freedom of expression is true. The Church of England has not been prevented from speaking its mind despite the efforts of politicians to muffle the voice. I think it is worth noting, however, that some of this freedom springs from other sources. It is generally agreed that the national Falkland Islands service was a turning point in church-state relations. The Archbishop of Canterbury, in a splendidly thoughtful sermon, set a tone of sorrow, relief and hope for the nation. But it was Dr Kenneth Greet, who was participating for the Free Churches, who ensured from the outset that thanksgiving for a military victory would have no place in the service. It was indeed a blow against chauvinistic religion.

The final argument discussed by Dr Habgood is that of ecumenism. Does the current form of establishment hinder church unity? The answer given is that it does not, since there are no plans for the formal organic union of the churches in England, and the specialized characters of all the churches will long be needed. I am not fully persuaded by this line of argument. If the Church of England is un-unitable-with, as I would judge it to be in the current form of establishment, then this indicates some malfunction within the body of Christ. Distinctive talents, yes. But a tie to the state which prevents ties with other churches, no.

I therefore believe that there are further questions which must be pressed within the Church of England, simply because the answers are by no means clear and the arguments are not all on one side. I believe there is a case for change. Could it be towards the Scottish model? There we have the public and parliamentary recognition that there is a national church, in which the monarch is a member, but which is free from parliamentary control. At first it appears to have the advantages of establishment – a public voice, access to the state system, a deep sense of responsibility – without the great disadvantage of Prime Ministerial power over its selection of senior officers. But it is not quite so perfect a solution. One of the most notable characteristics of established churches is their inability to change. They become part of the scenery. Like Edinburgh Castle, the Church of Scotland is recognizable in the national silhouette. Thus it becomes a prisoner of the conservationists. In fact, its freedom to change is limited by that mass opinion which is barely Christian at all, and which is articulated by the leader writers of the Scottish *Daily Express*. Those with knowledge, faith, experience and vision are constrained by those for whom the church is indeed a valued institution, but valued because they never attend it. In an Orthodox church, which believes everything that we need of God's truth is already given in its traditions, this may not be crucial. It sits very awkwardly indeed with a Reformed church which professes constant reformation.

The greatest gift that any national church offers is a permanent call to the eternal values of the Gospel set in the heart of public life. Its presence is a challenge to short-term politics, to the party see-saw, to bureaucratic tyrants, to economic self-delusion. It reminds those in power that 'this night shall your soul be required of you'. Every church is given the same Gospel, but the national church can project it in ways not open to smaller churches.

The greatest damage done by the national church in England has been indiscriminate baptism. This, far more than any complaint about privilege, has hindered unity in faith. For it has surrendered the meaning of faith and encouraged religion as a social custom, tinged with superstition, to usurp discipleship. A quasi-membership of the church then becomes a prophylactic against any real commitment of heart and mind. I believe it is a relic of medieval thinking which sees baptism as a tribal rite of passage and not a trumpet call of faith.

While there are many varieties of national church, the particular establishment in law which still continues in England requires a tripod support if it is to be sustained in the future. The legs are a population in which the great majority is Christian, a parliament in which the great majority is Christian, and a church which represents the great majority of Christians. The national establishment can survive the loss of one leg for a long time, the loss of two for a period, but when all three have gone there is no convincing basis for the ancient pattern. We are left with a splendid history and a dream of national unity and that damaging sense that the golden age of the church of God was in the past. So while I acknowledge the risks involved in any major movement (and nonconformists cannot ignore them), I believe the case for a deep, hard look at the establishment is a strong one.

Nevertheless, we must be realists too and recognize that neither in Scotland nor in England is the national church likely to propose change which would have the appearance of weakening its position in society. Can we suggest those areas in which current status can still be of value? The first I would put forward is the care of minorities which are so easily submerged in modern technological society. The responsibility of the national church is never self-preservation but a continuous watchman's rôle to alert the nation on behalf of those who can raise only a small voice themselves. Past history is not happy at

47

this point. A national church can resent religious minorities or try to ignore them. But we live in a very mixed society which holds diverse ideals and faiths. If we are to respect each person's individuality, if we are to learn from the insights of others, and if human rights are to be public policy number one, then the national church will lead the national search for justice.

Second, I would hope that a national church will refuse to be tied down to a nationalist faith. We honour Bishop George Bell of Chichester who demonstrated, at personal cost, that even in time of war the church is leaping over the barriers of enmity. He was not greatly supported or admired at the time. For it is during a national crisis that the national church is most drawn towards an interpretation of faith in the colour of the national flag. Yet Christ's church is always greater than the national expression of it. It is seeded throughout humanity and points to the essential unity of all in creation and in redemption.

Third, we can look towards national churches for a generous ecumenism. Their own place is secure. It is buttressed by property and inheritance and custom. So they are in a strong position to share in the search for the wholeness of the church and the unity of its witness which is at the heart of the ecumenical movement. The large churches in Germany have made very generous contributions to the World Council of Churches, but have not always made much progress in inter-church relations at home. The Catholic church in Italy and Spain has been in the rearguard of ecumenism. In Britain the national churches have not yet offered the fullness of their resources to the ecumenical movement. There are some who still cherish the notion that ecumenism means opening their arms and crying, 'Come back to mother.' Great things could happen if our national churches deliberately sought to offer facilities to others, to learn from others and to provide a generous umbrella for those of different churchmanship. I once heard Philip Potter, at the World Council of Churches, declare that no church had so great resources as the Church of England, but had used them to so little effect. It was a harsh word, perhaps indicating ecumenical frustration (a well-known professional disease), but with a glimmer of truth.

Finally, we must always expect from a nationally established church a concern for the national missionary enterprise. If the language of the church has become distant from the language of the people, has the established church helped us? When we lost intimate contact with the burgeoning industrial society, why was it necessary for Methodism to appear when the Church of England had all the facilities at hand? And why was poverty in our cities not a cause for action long before the publication of *Faith in the City*? The enormous weight of the missionary task – in terms of intellectual challenge, community support and personal evangelism – requires from us all a wholehearted dedication, and from our two great national churches a strategic commitment of people, plant, experience, prayer and money.

CHAPTER SEVEN

Minority Churches

The passions of the Reformation search for reality led to a form of separated churchmanship which has been with us ever since. It is not possible for us now to describe such division as sin. It may indeed be the fact that only by division could there be witness to a vital truth of the Gospel. But to remain content with division is surely a sign of our sin. In every generation we are called to remedy those defects in fellowship, understanding, doctrine or habit which still hinder the full unity of Christians. We remain, in the Protestant world, denominationally labelled. That is our mark of identity, the public sign of something distinctive in our approach to God or awareness of him. It is also a mark of our fellowship circle in which we operate and feel at home. For these reasons there can be an unhealthy clannishness in the life of minority churches in Europe, a defensiveness, a desire to wave a flag which arises from sociology rather than from the Gospel.

But at their best the minority churches have done very significant work for the nation. In France, for example, the Reformed churches have played an invaluable role in rescuing Christianity from a very heavily clericalized Catholicism. In England, the social awareness of Methodism and the Salvation Army has offered healing in the areas of human need that the larger churches too easily ignored. The Baptist, Congregational and Presbyterian traditions provided local training in responsibility during the eighteenth and nineteenth centuries when the political authorities gave little respect to those outside the establishment. All can record such contributions with thankfulness, and no one can now take that history away.

The particular theological emphasis that is retained by each denomination is a facet of the whole and therefore of permanent value. It is less easy to see the national relationship of the minority churches, since parliamentary disabilities have disappeared. A current risk is that in seeking a national rôle these churches will be preoccupied with making claims for themselves and pretending that the nineteenth century struggles for recognition have still to be fought. In Scotland and England, voices are raised about the lack of publicity for the minorities while the national churches are fully reported by press and radio. In England this leads some to seek a renewed importance for the Free Churches as a group. There are still public bodies which find it convenient to treat the Church of England, the Roman Catholics and the Free Churches as the sum total of Christianity in England –despite the fact that this omits great areas of Christian life: the Orthodox, the Lutherans, the black-led churches, the Quakers and the pentecostal groups. Some Free Churches tend to seek an old glory this way. There is a desire to present the 'Free Church voice' on issues of the day. But it is doubtful whether such a process is possible or desirable. There is not one Free Church ecclesiology but several, not one Free Church opinion on social morality but many, not one ordering of ministry. There are varied Free Church patterns of worship, from the formally liturgical to guitars and choruses. And if we say that all are indeed one in rejecting state authority in church affairs, then we have to include the Roman Catholics, and that does not suit the category at all.

The compelling identity of the historic Free Churches in England was formed by their struggle against a state-imposed religion and for an evangelical faith. We cannot recreate the freedom struggle, though there are signs that some Free Church people would like to do this by making a bogey out of the local Anglican bishop, just as a man who was once a nervous schoolboy and who feels lost without that authoritarian master in the neighbourhood, recreates the image in his wife. The powerful association of churches today is not any historical memory but their mutual commitment and calling to a common sacrificial witness in our secularized society. If a denomination is to use its historical treasures to the full, then it must share them in the ecumenical fellowship of churches, to help shape the patterns of Christian community for the future. My conviction is that our history is never so important as our future, for that is the meaning of forgiveness. It is in our shaping of the future life of the church, the kind of unity it will display, the leadership it will need, the resources it can deploy, that we fulfil our inheritance. So I do not see the national witness of the Free Churches as a block vote which corrects the Church of England. I look towards service to the national community in many ways, of which the following are critical:

1. To love freedom and to recognize the limits of freedom. As Christians we rejoice that the Holy Spirit leads us into truth – in our thinking, praying and action. We are free to follow that leading. But

any community life limits freedom. We limit what we may do because we wish to be part of a society which decides there are many things we may not do. As churches, we are limited both to our own constitutions which reflect our reading of the Gospel, and by the law of the land. It has surprised many people to discover that in some respects the Church of England has a freedom in law which is denied to the Free Churches. For example, when we have sought to modernize the language of the marriage service we find the Church of England can do this by the actions of the General Synod, but the Free Churches may not because they are bound by the Marriage Act and any amendment of that awaits the co-operation of the government. When we have looked for ways of passing a piece of church property to a sister church, we find that the Church of England may freely decide the sale price or the rent. But Free Churches are bound by the Charities Act and have to sell to the highest bidder, so that a black-led church is always at a disadvantage when it seeks accommodation in this way. Freedom is never absolute.

The love and the limits of freedom belong together. In the background we recall how the love of freedom inspired the parliamentary uprising against the king in the seventeenth century, but the limits were then soon discovered and enforced by Cromwell in power. Before that, we may remember a famous paradox of Luther, 'A Christian man is the most free lord of all, and subject to none; a Christian man is the most dutiful servant of all, and subject to everyone.' And so we go back to the one who was both servant and lord, free from the bondage of the law yet bound to the cross. It is this combination of liberty and discipline which is an offering by the minority churches to the life of the nation at a period when those two factors are popularly regarded as enemies. The more highly the Christian community values its freedom, to design its own worship and life, the more it needs to subordinate individual taste and fashion to the sense of fellowship. Otherwise freedom becomes an ego trip. This pattern stands in public life as a sign of community in the Gospel.

2. To honour the unity of the church of Christ. The exercise of freedom has, in the history of the church, led to many breaks in the fabric, many schisms, many bitter arguments. There have been times when Roman Catholics have said that this is the key quality of Protestantism, and is beyond healing. We are grateful for all the movements in this century to correct the tendency to division, movements which never win easy acceptance because they challenge long-established ways of thought, but which seek faithfulness to the prayer of Christ. There are different possibilities for different places,

and we cannot assume that one model of unity will apply everywhere. Nowhere have we found a perfect road. The union of Protestants in South and North India has been a shining light for many of us, but even there groups hostile to the unions have managed to entangle the church in legal battles which damage its witness. Each union leaves somebody out, some passion unsatisfied, some concept unfulfilled. This is why unity is so hard a process in the church, for even as we embrace new colleagues with the kiss of peace we may have to see an old friend go out of the door, and to make decisions with such results is very hard for us.

Yet it is necessary too. The character of our society in Britain with the widespread breakdown in marriage, the alienation of so many young people through unemployment, the amorality of the financial community, the continued influence of racism – all this requires so dedicated and intelligent a witness to Christ that the denominational labels lose much of their old significance and we are drawn together to pool talents for the sake of the nation. This has happened in many localities, and I am grateful that my own small denomination has been in the forefront of the process to establish, authorize and encourage local ecumenical projects. This is a peculiarly English road towards Christian unity, very patchy and diverse, but dedicated to the local witness of faithful people. We cannot see the end of the process but we know the denominations are changing through these local schemes, and we trust that the road of greater fellowship is God's way even though we do not yet see the destination.

The smaller Protestant denominations are given the freedom to move into unity if they are convinced a particular change is right. The Church of England has a more difficult process, for not only does its General Synod retain a voting pattern by houses which means that one third plus one of the clergy alone can defeat any scheme, but major change will also have to be approved by Parliament. The Roman Catholic church also has great difficulty, since one part of the church, even if heartily convinced about a movement into unity, has to await more general movement and this may mean that Holland, for example, has to wait for Spain. The convoy is slow indeed. The Free Churches and those other smaller bodies which have autonomy therefore carry a very considerable responsibility to challenge the barriers that still remain between people who are following the one Christ.

3. To be communities of conviction. In Britain today there is not much left of the old customary support for church life. What remains is mainly dedicated to the Church of England which deliberately and

conscientiously seeks to hold residual folk religion within its embrace, believing that even fragmentary traces of belief are always to be encouraged. The Free Churches do not have that constituency. It is true that not all the members have a lively or educated conviction about Christian doctrine. Many of us have entered a particular church because of the accident of birth rather than by open choice. But in the main it is true that people do not become members except by conviction, and do not remain in fellowship unless there is genuine spiritual help found there.

Such communities are necessary for our national health. Their existence speaks of the drawing power of Christ and the personal cost involved when we join the community of Christ. Not many of our church buildings are so lovely nor their decoration so imaginative that we are drawn for aesthetic reasons. Today there are not many people attracted by the eloquence of the preacher. The maintenance of local centres of worship and local ministry is a costly business. All these factors reduce any social reason for coming together, and the reduction in local church membership rolls so evident in the last fifty years is partly because of this change in climate. So conviction is a major element in forming each local church outside the parish system of the two national churches. It is conviction about the centrality of Christ, the simplicity of our approach to him and the responsibility we each carry for living out the faith. It is conviction, too, about the essential equality of all as we face the challenge of the cross. It is conviction that God's good purposes, shown us in Christ, are the world's hope and salvation. To have thousands of places where such conviction creates community (however marred by all our human inadequacy and meanness) is to participate in bringing health to our nation. For it is a constant witness to values and realities largely neglected in Britain today. The search for instant satisfaction and excitement, the acceptance of impersonal 'market forces', the judgment of success and failure by bank balance, and the repeated complaint that other people are always to blame – such characteristics are constantly challenged by conviction churches. I believe that in the unity which the Lord will give to his church there will be a place not only for the territorial unit but for the conviction unit. Both reflect aspects of the Gospel which are precious.

4. To co-operate for social justice. We have noted that the nationally established churches have an entry into the world of politics which is both a privilege and a responsibility. The smaller churches have just as much on their conscience but have no escalator into the board room. But the smaller churches do have freedom, and can take a

public position without causing a parliamentary storm. The risk is plain. There is a constant temptation to make pronouncements on public issues which salve the conscience but have no visible effect on government, press, commerce or the social services. This is sometimes called 'putting down a marker' or 'staking out the ground' or even 'conscientization'. Churches cannot ignore injustice or violence. The lesson the smaller churches have learnt is that co-operative research and action is essential if they are to be effective in this field. Perhaps it is optimistic to say that they have learnt this. There are occasions when they forget it. But the learning process goes on and there are fewer Free Church people today who would attempt a denominational assault on the Departments of State.

Increasingly, therefore, these Protestant churches have valued the co-ordinating role of the British Council of Churches. Working together means that each participant may get rather less than the particular aim of that church, but ensures a careful hearing from major public institutions. In a quite distinctive position, the Roman Catholic church has not so far thrown its weight into co-operative public witness but has used both its considerable British resources and its international expertise to press its own social concerns. It will add greatly to the strength of public Christian witness when the Roman Catholic church fully engages with Protestants and the Orthodox in regular study and action on social issues. Of course there are strains to live with in such co-operative work, but to present a public plea or challenge or hope from all the churches is a most effective method.

We discovered this on a topic which was in a minor key, not one of the life and death issues of our day, the issue of Sunday trading. It happened that on this issue many interests came together and formed a temporary alliance. There were 'evangelical' Christians who felt called to hold to a sabbatarian interpretation of scripture; there were liberal Christians out to defend shop workers from exploitation; there were urban householders who feared a week without respite from the crowds and noise and church people who thought worship on Sunday would be threatened. None wanted to preserve the existing chaos of legislation, but none agreed with the policy of total de-regulation put forward by the government. We waited, as the saying goes, on the Home Secretary, but he declared that no compromise could work or could be considered. There was a widespread campaign to write to Members of Parliament. The result was a defeat of the government on a government bill – the only one during the 1983/7 Parliament with its large Conservative majority.

A large degree of co-operative witness has been possible on other issues. On South Africa and sanctions policy the smaller churches and the national churches have been at one, but have failed to move Britain as a whole towards an activist policy. On immigration there has been a great deal of good casework on disputed rights for individuals, but again little effect on national policy. The broad issue of development aid to the poorest parts of the world has been very faithfully pressed by the dual technique of public education and pressure, and through the churches doing a great deal of effective transmission of aid themselves. A major exercise in public pressure was a mass lobby of Parliament which did have the effect of lifting the subject of overseas aid higher up the political agenda, though never high enough to win the full parliamentary support it needs. United pressure towards action which will build a more just world can be inspired by minority churches.

5. To be self-critical in the light of the Word of God. These smaller denominations which have sprung out of the Reformation are committed to continual search for the living Word, Jesus Christ, in the words of men and women, words written in scripture and lived in contemporary life. There is no guarantee that, in such a community, we shall always be right, but there is the assurance that the Lord will guide if only we will listen and obey. Churches with that fundamental belief can afford to launch out, to confess sins, to discard old ideas, to rejoice in their young people, to accept their own fallibility. Constant reformation is no easy road. There is a lot of pain involved in self-criticism, and a danger of becoming self-absorbed. It is worth noting here that when a nation follows this path, we often forget our idealism. China, during the Cultural Revolution, was looking for ways in which the initial impetus of revolution which created the People's Republic could be repeated, the same enthusiasms generated and the same disciplines evoked. To those of us outside, it seemed a backward step. We are more at ease with the pragmatic state, trimming its ideology as economics may demand and ignoring the seismic idealism of the past. But the churches of the Reformation cannot rest on one historic shift. They can only rest on the contemporary knowledge of God given by the Holy Spirit, however hard it may be to receive and accept. This is why, although they produce statements of belief, they refuse to be for ever bound by them, for no form of words, written by people of limited vision and with ideas culturally conditioned, can preserve fully the life of the Spirit.

Such churches have a dynamic relation to the society in which they live. They can never become simple accepters of a status quo, partners with government whatever its colour, imitators of other public institutions, swallowers of party dogma, propagandists for the latest craze. Always they will be looking for the otherness of God in the midst of human struggles, listening for that word of redemption and hope for the mediocrity of public life, and offering a critical friendship to those who become powerful in politics and commerce. If they are faithful, they will not surrender their heart to any ideology. So, while a nationally established church is tempted to play the Vicar of Bray, the minority Protestant churches are tempted to take on the colour of a perpetual opposition party, playing the 'outsider' card. It is a risk worth taking.

CHAPTER EIGHT

Patriotism and Protest

I once heard D. T. Niles, a great ecumenical gift from the Methodist church in Sri Lanka, comment that although the church is never *of* the nation, it is *for* the nation; 'if it is not for the nation then what on earth is it for?' At a time of immense effort in nation building, he was affirming the rôle the church must play. It is not a casual bystander. By prayer and life and exhortation and hopefulness, the Christian community is alongside those who give their all to create a nation out of the rubble of war or the disintegration of empires. That is simply patriotism. But patriotism is seldom so simple.

There is something almost instinctive about loving our own country. In some places patriotism is instilled by a vast propaganda machine, with endless parades of the flag and chanting of the anthem, with pictures of the nation's leaders on every street and regular public appearances of the head of state. That can become a brain-washing technique. It is strange that anyone regards the expenditure as necessary, for there can be very few people who do not care deeply for the country of their birth without all these devices. We cannot escape the sense that our country is important even when we believe it is mistaken; we would rather be at home than abroad, even if home means a grubby city; and to hear our country reviled hurts us even if there is some truth in the criticism. No, what the official flag wavers are after is not a simple basic patriotism, but rather support for the regime in power and the wiping from our minds of all its follies, errors and mischief. The more patriotism is boosted by the authorities, the more carefully we should ask who has been locked up and who has recently been widowed and where the generals get their orders.

For this is the point where patriotism is most at risk in the modern world, not by people losing their lifelong love of their country, but through manipulation by authorities which elevate national security into a religion. It is a contagious sickness. 'The state is threatened' really means 'I and my party are threatened', and then 'serve your country' comes to mean 'betray the political opposition'. Of course this duplicity is not universal, and we can think of instances where national security has indeed been at stake in the sense that the nation would have died by takeover if the opposition had not been firmly dealt with. The Communist insurrection in Malaysia, the Mau Mau in Kenya and the IRA in Ulster may come to mind. But how hard it is to single out the honest clear-eyed response to a wholly unworthy subversion and the use of national sentiment by a ruling caste. Our judgments usually depend on our political views. The true patriot is the one who agrees with us.

We see this displayed in a tragic way in South Africa. Government patriotism means tacit or vocal support for the regime, acceptance that it knows best, willingness to see racialism go on for years, decades; it means connivance in the division of the country between the tribes and the closing of eyes to police brutality. Patriotism for members of the ANC or SWAPO means loving the country enough to fight for its release from an evil regime, suffering patiently even to death, refusing to temporize, training, educating, hoping and the closing of eyes to guerrilla brutality. So we point to the true patriot according to our view of what is the heart and purpose of the nation. At the time I am writing, the debate in the United States about the Iran/*contra* affair has filled the North American media, and it is clear that those who support the US President constantly refer to Nicaraguan Freedom Fighters, while opponents speak of the *contras*. This is probably a piece of public relations, but it could also be a genuine difference of vision. It is possible to view the same people, on the borders of Nicaragua, as brave refugees struggling to win back their country from a Marxist takeover, and as a gang of dispossessed middle class people who failed utterly to win power through the electoral system and so resort to terror. This factor alone renders patriotism a complex passion. It is a mixture of what is necessary for me and my future, and what is sought by the majority of my fellow citizens and what my government decrees.

So the church cannot have an easy task when patriotism is questioned. In the early years of the apostolic church, while Christian disciples were a small fringe group in the Roman empire, Christians were suspect. They were not ready to pledge total loyalty to the emperor and were not ready to fight the emperor's wars. They called another their Lord. Part of the persecution mania of some Roman emperors grew out of a fear that subversives were tunnelling into the foundations of the state, and Christians could be counted in that number. Whenever duty and loyalty have been construed in terms of total obedience to one man, then Christians have been placed in great difficulty. The major development into nationalism meant that in place of that one figurehead the nation itself became the entity which all were destined to serve. This shift was made plain by the parliamentary revolt against Charles I in England. After long and painful debate, the conclusion was stated that loyalty did not prevent accusing, trying, judging and executing the king since the king was not the realm, the nation. Patriotism is love of the country, not of its ruler.

Yet the growth of the modern nation state, with its vast powers, raises much the same dilemma as the autocrats of old and the dictators of today. The shape of government varies, but the power to educate, inform, bully, tax, commandeer, keep secrets, pass emergency powers, reward friends, engineer alliances and build bombs is present in the great majority. Where such power is misused, Christians may believe it is right to rebel. That will always be an extreme position, not easily reached. But within my own tradition of churchmanship, with that Puritan militancy in our heritage, I cannot rule out the just rebellion. It is a position painfully discovered by many Christians in our generation. Three modern examples of protest, though not rebellion, come from East Asia.

It is a part of the world unaccustomed to democracy. Overlords have been common: kings, warlords, generals. To look solely through European eyes is therefore to twist the picture. Yet in the Philippines, South Korea and Taiwan the Christian community has led movements aimed at greater democratic choice against all the established power of tough regimes.

In the Philippines, it was the Roman Catholic church which took a major share in the popular movement which led to the flight of President Marcos. Looking back we can see that corruption, seeping through all the offices of state and defended by military power, led to a disenchantment and a boiling frustration. Even a brief visit to the grim back streets of Manila provides an inescapable indictment of the luxury enjoyed by the powerful. The uprising did not mirror the civil war which has been continuous in a sporadic way in many islands. It was never an armed attack on the government. The church played a major role in ensuring a peaceful protest as priests and nuns took an active place in the processions, revealing their clerical dress, leading hymns and prayers. It was a big risk. The church could have taken a judicial back seat. A good many clergy, especially in senior positions, were inclined that way. But today the real patriotism of the church is lauded for its activity in the great protest.

Similarly in South Korea the churches, both Catholic and Protestant, have backed the 1987 demonstrations against the regime. The Presbyterian churches, in particular, have long crusaded for civil rights. They have investigated cases of political torture, of deaths in police custody, and have campaigned for a free press and democratic elections. A number of leading figures have been imprisoned. It is a story of faithfulness against a seemingly impregnable regime. Poised in a geographical location so close to a disputed border, the government has always been able to label opposition as 'friends of the Communists' and to bludgeon them accordingly. Any radical social movement could be so painted. This might have caused Christian caution. But the reverse is what happened. The more the regime waved its anti-Communist flag, the more the church knew that the government had no basis in reason for its declaration. It was trying to bluff the world. So the church took a leading part, along with the university students, in the tempestuous days which squeezed concession after concession from the president's men.

A very different situation in Taiwan has caused another Presbyterian church to take a consciously opposition stance. The government since 1949 has been in the hands of the mainland Chinese who, following Chiang Kai Shek, left home at the Communist takeover. Before that, the island experienced a long spell of Japanese rule. So it seemed to the native people of the island that they were exchanging one set of expatriate rulers for another; they, the majority, had very little say. The mainlanders, known as the KMT or Kuo Ming Tang party, rule in Taipei as the Government of China in exile, and acknowledge the island itself as only one of all the provinces of China which they, in name only, represent. Add to that a military style of government dedicated to the 'recovery of the mainland' with thirty-eight years of martial law. Add to that the self-interest of the great powers, always ready to forget the people of Taiwan in favour of an embassy in Beijing. It is a tough context for patriotism. The Presbyterian church, the main Protestant community, established long before the KMT era, has published a series of statements 'regarding our national fate', calling attention to the right of these fifteen million people to decide their own destiny, to form their own government, to act without duress. This has meant continual handicap through administrative pressure, and the imprisonment of the General Secretary of the church. The government has regularly tried to engineer disunity in the church's General Assembly. It still regards free political debate on 'our national fate' as a form of disloyalty, since everyone should know that the only destiny to be talked about is for China to be whole again with a KMT government in charge. It is amazing that for so many years a mirage can control the destiny of a country and only the absence of genuine political discussion and opposition can keep the mirage trembling before the public gaze, always attractive, always in the distance, always receding.

A superficial reading of such situations as these would suggest that patriotism is pressure which succeeds and disloyalty is pressure which fails. That is how it may appear, but we need to dig a little deeper. At the heart of patriotism is the identity of a people. We know ourselves in the world context as belonging to this particular nation with all its history and culture. That has been part of the very creation of our personality. Another part is the family and all we receive in that context. Being within the national family offers benefits and calls for duties. We cannot easily escape from either. We love the national family not primarily by obeying its current officers but by understanding and seeking its health, its unity, its creativeness, its offering to others. This is where the very concept of patriotism has been, and still is, traduced by people of great power, for they come to identify themselves as the nation. *L'état c'est moi* has been mouthed in many tongues by a great variety of dictators from the Emperor Bokassa to Papa Doc and Joseph Stalin. Black or white, right wing or left wing, snobs or peasants, the disease is the same, the total identity of the national good with what I want. This is evidently an encroaching temptation for national leaders even in more democratic regimes. Real patriotism cannot simply accept this trend and make the expected responses. On the contrary, it is fulfilled only through reasoned and careful opposition. Therefore it depends on a vision of the nation and its good, and it is precisely there that Christians can be expected to make a distinctive contribution, based on the witness of scripture that God loves justice, and on justice builds peace. That is a Jewish vision also.

> Is not this what I require of you as a fast:
>> to loose the fetters of injustice,
>> to untie the knots of the yoke,
>> to snap every yoke
>> and set free those who have been crushed?
> Is it not sharing your food with the hungry,
> taking the homeless poor into your house,
> clothing the naked when you meet them
> and never evading a duty to your kinsfolk?
> Then shall your light break forth like the dawn
> and soon you will grow healthy like a wound newly healed.
>> (Isaiah 58.6–8)

To this we add the presence of the Kingdom in the person of Jesus Christ, who himself lived out that sharing, vulnerable, yoke-snapping vision. To love our country means drawing it closer to the vision of what it is called to be.

Though all Christian groups in Britain – as indeed across the world – will claim to be patriotic in these terms, the record is not always one of concerted, conscientious, effective love of country. There is one group whose record is outstanding, the Society of Friends. These Christians have been unremitting in their effort to ask the hard questions about national policy and to give answers with their own lives. Their witness against war has been parallel to a willingness to serve all who are hurt by war. Although their pacifist view does not command universal assent among Christians, their utter commitment does win admiration, so that they can never be accused of a lack of patriotism. Individual Friends have sought to carry the anti-war witness into peace-time politics by refusing to pay that portion of income tax which is spent on armaments and military forces. The law has defeated them, and I believe for good reasons, for it appears to me impossible to hypothecate portions of tax for particular objects. But I admire the rigour of the moral conviction, that if it is evil to fire atomic bombs then it is evil also to build them, and we should not be party to what we know to be evil. Many Christians argue differently. They would say that in a world of great power, the only stance that can hold back the expansion of corrupt or oppressive regimes is to hold even greater power ourselves. They might further point to the pacifist position as an opting out of that tough political world where turning the other cheek has not yet stopped an aggressor. The argument goes on. But I am convinced that patriotism is best served by such a thoughtful probing of immensely hard choices rather than by the easy flag-waving of our popular press.

For most people, however, for most of the time patriotism is not a matter of crisis decision. It is a background element of life which does not need to be talked about. Our Christian faith does not depend on our nationality, nor our nationality on our faith. If patriotism and religion are fused, then the identity becomes so extreme, so intolerant, that we fear for basic human freedom, as in the Iran of the Ayatollah. At that extreme, patriotism excuses anything, however immoral. A patriot has plenary absolution. That is not a route for Christian states, nor individual Christians, because morality is not dependent on national interest. The openness of the United States' constitution ('Congress shall make no law respecting an establishment of religion, or prohibiting the free exercise thereof; or abridging the

63

freedom of speech, or of the press, or of the right of the people peaceably to assemble and to petition the Government for a redress of grievances' First Amendment) has in no way hindered a patriotic spirit, but has rather encouraged it as every variety of cultural and religious minority has been able to share equally in the national fortunes. A plural society certainly complicates social life, and enriches it. We can no longer claim a closed system of thought. Freedom tests us all.

But when that freedom is denied, and the great debates are silenced and the authorities claim that loyalty means their way alone, then the Christian community may be faced with the hardest choice of all, which is the possible route of violence. I noted that the Puritan inheritance makes it hard for me to rule out this possibility. It is hard, in any case, for general statements to have much validity. It is only by living with a particular regime that Christians can come to a decision, even though they may be helped by a host of friends elsewhere. The current issue which is most often before us is South Africa and the choice which black Christians are being called to make about acceptance of the present regime, or that hard opposition which may well have violence at its edge. As we listen and pray with our friends, it is good to remember that for nearly two hundred years the churches of Britain have had this issue placed before them. Early Protestant missionaries, Vanderkemp and Philip, wrote scathing reports of white attitudes in the first decades of the nineteenth century. When Philip was taken to court in Cape Town and fined for his publications, it was British churches which raised the money and paid the fine. Two hundred years of inadequate education, two hundred years of the poorest-paid jobs, two hundred years of abasement before the boss, two hundred years of the shanty-town life on the edge of an expanding economy, two hundred years of patience. What then can we say about forbearance and finding a reasonable way through discussion? How can we urge that the parliamentary process be respected? What would we expect black people to reply when a proud, powerful government says, 'Give us time'? I cannot believe that loving our country means accepting an evil system for ever, and though the route of violence challenges the way of the cross, there may indeed be occasions when Christians can find no alternative. We must do everything to find that alternative, for we know that violence is not hallowed, it is not what God wills for us, it is not living now within the Kingdom. How strange then that in Britain and the European Community and the United States there has been so great a reluctance to deal with South Africa through very tough sanctions. It has been almost as though our governments have said, 'We cannot approve apartheid, but we will not take non-violent measures to overthrow it. So let violence decide the outcome.' Economic pressure may not work, but we are wholly committed to seek every alternative to civil war.

This leads us inevitably to consider how love of our country moves out beyond the geographical limits and becomes part of our care for humanity. We start where we are, where we belong, and with the identity given to us. But the world is changing, and we are already seeing changes in the status of the nation.

CHAPTER NINE

The World Parish

During the eighteenth century the Euopean development of international trade and the evangelistic outlook of Christians took on their modern pattern. It was not a very well-planned process, nor a very holy one. Within it the slave trade was, so to speak, the bottom line, revealing the worst excesses of unfettered capitalism tied to colonial power. At the other extreme, the early attempts at Christian mission were visionary, in that they were boldly staking out a world claim for Christ at a time when the task was far beyond human resources. When the known world was growing ever wider and more complex, the Christian church had to re-order its concept of boundaries. This was a painful exercise for many who regarded the Christian faith as European faith. But it was a theological necessity, for if Christ was Lord at all then he was Lord for all and if God loved the world then no tribe or territory, no science or philosophy, no economic bubble, no national government could be outside that love. International relations between states, as distinct from the relationship between rulers, developed and have continued to grow more complex and more pressing ever since.

Now those elementary relations have grown into one of the most powerful agencies of human life – the impact of one nation on another. At every shop counter we meet the fruit of international trade. We cross international boundaries readily. We affect the lives of people far away by what we eat. Crime and terrorism slip across every frontier. The pacts between nations can create a common market or a common military force or a common intellectual exercise. A stroll around the institutional section of Geneva reveals how many international bodies now affect our lives, to forecast our weather or to examine our labour laws, or to protect authors' copyright or to seek peace on earth. Certainly the speed and ease of modern communications have brought home to us the immense possibilities of internationalism, but they frighten us too with the realization that there is a hungry world on our doorstep.

Isolation is no longer an option – a reality now accepted by the Chinese political leadership after two millennia of attempting to keep the walls intact. Isolation is not possible for the Soviet Union, despite the building of new walls, for the traffic of air waves and ideas, music and aircraft, nuclear cloud and medical craftsmanship cross and re-cross the boundaries. Neither is it a possibility for those little island communities in the south Pacific, once protected by a thousand miles of ocean. Today the tourists fly in and the nuclear tests continue, and nationalism batters at the last colonial outposts. Since no nation lives alone, there is no such thing as total national autonomy. We depend on what we can sell, and that depends on what others are able to buy. They need not buy from us; we become dependent. We depend on what we can buy. If the oil price shoots up, as it did in the 1970s, then our economy is affected regardless of the policy of our government. A frost in Brazil, a plant disease in Ghana, a blight in the vineyards and the international commodity markets tremble. This inter-dependence of the nations is rarely recognized by politicians when they come to us seeking our vote. Then they appear as masters of the manifesto, crammed with ability to make decisions. In fact, the national government is very often responsive to factors over which it has no control at all.

To some, this is a hopeful reality. To many, however, it is a damaging and wholly unwelcome discovery. When a nation has struggled towards independence over many years, and has at last seen its own flag raised over the castle and has installed its first home-grown government in the senate house, the expectation is that policy will be made at home. The discovery that many of the great decisions will be made elsewhere is a shock. This leads to charges of a new imperialism. It may be so, but not in the same manner as the old, for it is no longer one or two imperial powers which alone are autonomous. All are interdependent. What differs is the degree rather than the principle.

A few years ago, the primary agent blamed for stealing away national autonomy was the transnational corporation. These commercial and industrial giants have had the power to develop major plants in many locations, drawing back much of the ultimate benefit to the shareholders, and, as foreigners, shaping the industrial revolution in many parts of the third world. They are extraordinarily difficult to pin down. Like some wealthy octopus, there are always limbs where least expected, subsidiaries with odd names, clinging to another part of the world's flesh. Because of this it has been hard to discover how policy is made, and all too easy to hide a commercial imperialism. But there is another side to this story which radical Christians have readily forgotten. The incoming commercial company never has an entirely free hand, for national governments can set the terms for leasing land, developing natural resources, paying tax, sharing management responsibility. The impetus of imported capital may be an essential trigger for other, more local, development. The effects of the transnational corporations are therefore not all on one side of the balance. The tragedy has been that too often they have used their power without regard to local aspirations, and that poor national governments have not been able to challenge them. There is a considerable change taking place now.

The transnational corporations are becoming less powerful on the world scene as the finance houses become more powerful. Even great industrial giants are vulnerable. They can suddenly find that the vast amount of money needed for new investment is not there, or that a takeover bid rocks their stability. They are learning to be diplomatically patient in socialist countries, faced with governments which will supervise them closely. But the finance houses have remarkable freedom, for they are concerned with dealing in money, not in goods. They can transfer assets from one currency to another at the touch of a computer button. Their only output is a remarkable balance sheet of winners and losers. They acknowledge no morality beyond profit, and in this they mirror some of the great industrial companies. At a recent Annual General Meeting, the Chairman of British Airways was asked why the firm continued to fly to South Africa. He replied, 'We are not here to make moral judgments. We are here to make profits for the shareholders.' Financiers of the world, applaud the frankness of such a spokesman! But let us beware the amoral engine which is driving so much of the world's economy for, like patriotism, profit can excuse anything.

This is the darker side of international village politics. We all know that there is some better news. International medical research, new ways of helping the physically and mentally handicapped, co-operative response to major disasters, the international eye on criminals and terrorists, the genesis of mutual action to save our flora and fauna – all these and many more are facets of the interactive world, pointing a way forward for the human family. It is an easy pastime to ridicule international organizations. The surprising thing is how much genuine idealism remains when the rhetoric of national politics threatens to drown practical planning. The internationalists are in the van of the next great shift in human society, towards the full acceptance of international law and the international conservation of scarce world resources, towards the pooling of both markets and productive ideas.

But is not the Christian church in the van of such a movement? Its origin and its faith impel it to be international. The answer has to be that more often than not it has been satisfied to be national. To look at the positive aspect first, we recognize in the Roman Catholic church a sustained and formidable attempt to hold the international dimension as crucial for its life. At no period has it been content to be called the Roman church. However, the Italian character of the Vatican secretariat has for centuries been a question mark placed alongside the catholic basis. It is not easy to retain a good geographical spread of the most senior clergy, though recent observers report that there is real progress here. Universal in the teaching of the faith, universal in the character of its worship and universal in acceptance of a central authority. It is a signal and a challenge. No one brought up within the smaller groupings of Protestantism can fail to thank God for the bridge-building quality which enables Catholics to hold an identity far beyond that of nationalism.

There are some questions to be asked from recent experience. The first concerns the treatment given by the Vatican to liberation theologians in Latin America. Here was a case where a particular context of the one Catholic church has called forth a particular faith response. It has been a response of head and heart. Both strong intellectual work and co-operative living and striving have been involved. All the theology has been prayed through and lived out. This does not mean that it should have automatic acceptance elsewhere, for what grows out of that context of poverty cannot be transplanted easily. But it does mean that a truly international church would listen and learn and love, even when there are hesitations. The action of the Vatican in branding some Catholic theologians as Marxist showed a narrowness of understanding and, I believe, a failure to read their work objectively. I think this was particularly true in the case of Leonardo Boff. It is not enough for a universal church to rejoice in the drumming of Africans and the dancing of Polynesians, it also has to allow the Holy Spirit to speak through the diverse experience of humanity.

My second question is whether the universal character has yet been used fully to help forward reconciliation between nations. It is a hard question, because, by the very nature of things, so much of the international diplomacy is carried out very quietly. My experience was in seeking to build friendship between British and Argentine

69

Christians after the Falkland Islands fighting. Much was done between Protestant churches on both sides. But in Argentina those churches are a small minority, and it was important to engage the Roman Catholic church in the same work. This proved very hard to do. The two hierarchies were reluctant to engage in a serious programme of reconciliation because, so we were told, all such contacts are handled by the Vatican. Those are the 'proper channels'. Are they fully open?

My third question is whether Roman Catholic theology has been led, by the very fact of universality, to adopt universal moral judgments when diversity might better reveal the love of the Father for his children. I recognize the power and the teaching dynamic of absolutist statements. But when the result of this is, for example, to oppose family planning in Bangladesh, then the law has become a rod to beat our humanity. It places a theoretical assurance (that contraception is immoral) above the practical certainty that more lives in that country will mean worse lives. Life means quality and not only quantity. It is not only a word describing biological activity but holds within it meaning, purpose, growth, awareness, rhythm, expectation. By declaring one universal, divine and natural law, the Roman theologians have dismissed the primacy of people in favour of cells. It is a shift only possible for those who habitually think in terms of law.

These are serious questions, but they are posed against the background of the one Christian institution which has deliberately practised internationalism throughout its history. Protestantism can make no such claim. Growing up during the era of rising nationalism, the churches fitted themselves into the new boundaries with no sense of restriction. It has become axiomatic that Protestant churches are defined by the nation in which they live. When boundaries change, so do churches. When East Pakistan became Bangladesh, the United Church of Pakistan was also split. When Malaysia and Singapore separated, the Presbyterian church divided too. The exceptions to this rule are brave and rare. One is the United Congregational Church of Southern Africa, boldly retaining its united life in Zimbabwe, Botswana, Namibia, Mozambique and the Republic. To me, a sad break in fellowship was that in Samoa. For over a hundred years there was one Congregational church bridging all the Samoan islands. Politics have separated Eastern Samoa as a United States territory from Western Samoa as an independent nation. A few years ago, the church split despite the unities of language and culture which still tie the islands together.

Over the centuries this limitation has shaped the Protestant mind so that a national label has become characteristic. It means that all the key decisions are taken within that framework. The result is plain. The international dimension of the church has been pushed to the edge of church life and thought, and so there is a constant struggle to give it any place at all. There are several ways in which Protestants have sought to retain an international dimension.

The characteristic nineteenth century mode was the missionary society which created awareness, enthusiasm and sacrificial giving. It was a primary educating force. It was once said that civil servants in the Foreign Office in London probably knew less about the world than did the staffs of the missionary societies. The commitment of resources to world evangelization was a true reflection of the Gospel dynamic, and it effected the most rapid spread of Christianity in history. Born out of evangelical conviction, there was also a political connection which coloured the whole enterprise, for the missionaries and the empire builders travelled the same roads, taught the same aspects of civilization and only occasionally confessed to major differences of principle. The story was heroic. No one today, crossing the globe with ease and listening to news on short-wave radio, can afford to belittle the achievements of missionary pioneers, achievements born out of faith, stamina and selflessness. The effect, however, has not been to put the international church at the centre of the Protestant vision. It has tended to affirm the nationalism and the racialism of many European Christians who still believe that it is their sort of faith which has to teach the world, while others are forever on the receiving end. The continuance of European and North American missionary societies to the end of the twentieth century is evidence of this. If we really believed in the international church and the essential equality of all its parts, then we would deal internationally church-to-church without any society as intermediary. To maintain these specialist bodies does not imply that they all follow outdated techniques or tired philosophies. On the contrary, they often display thoughtfulness and vigour with an awareness (particularly in the United States) of modern communication methods. But it is the actual existence of such bodies which suggests that 'we are the senders of the Gospel to the world'. Why cannot we learn to rejoice in the wonder of the Holy Spirit's work, that the church is now present in every country under heaven and, in each place, is the primary agent of the commision of Christ? Having served for many years through a missionary society, I can only rejoice that this measure of internationalism has been kept before the churches; but I regret the slowness in coming to terms with a very different world and a different task.

The second Protestant channel for internationalism is an offshoot of the first. As the European churches exported their understanding of Christ, so they sent a style of churchmanship. All the great Protestant divisions have a European origin – many of them in Britain. These separated traditions have become world-wide groupings of churches or communions which can act together. They are very varied in style. By far the most highly organized is the Lutheran World Federation, with a large central staff in Geneva and its own inter-church aid division. It exerts a good deal of influence and perhaps this is one reason why Lutheran churches find it so hard to enter into local unions with other Christians within the Reformation tradition. The other very significant grouping is the Anglican, for although there is autonomy for each Province, the tradition of leadership from Canterbury is still strong, and the inter-weaving of great theological variety with a vivid historical sense provides flexibility. Anglicans have not worked out in any formal way how their world communion can make decisions and this now causes concern, for Provincial differences are testing the unity of the fellowship. The Baptist, Methodist, Reformed and Disciples' groupings are less highly developed and see friendship and mutual encouragement as a large part of their basis. In no way have the local or national bodies ceded authority to these world bodies.

A major reason for the existence of world families of this sort is that they provide a partner in discussion for the Roman Catholic church. If the great theological issues of the Reformation are to be faced openly by both sides and steadily resolved, then the Vatican has to engage in dialogue. It therefore seeks to meet international groupings which represent the whole range of Protestant views. A series of dialogues is in process. Some major issues are being resolved. But it is important to note that an agreement reached by a gathering of scholars and theologians, though significant, may well not carry the mind of the international communion and is unlikely to carry the mind of all the local churches. It is simply the cutting of the barbed wire; whether anyone will then move through the opening is another question, a question of will.

A third strand of international agency is the Council of Churches, both regional and global. This is a more recent development and we are still learning how it fits beside the other two. It provides one essential the others lack – the full spectrum of churchmanship from Orthodox to Baptist, and from the small churches of the Pacific islands to the great Protestant bodies of the USA. Born out of world war sorrows, the World Council of Churches has inspired a network of inter-church aid and service to refugees. As it has grown over forty years, the white North-Atlantic churches have come to see that third world Christians are providing the dynamic of growth and the challenge of action. The WCC is never a comfortable haven. In the world confessional families it is possible to be so much at home with similar people that the sharpest issues do not arise. But I would testify that the reality of challenge, and thus of development, comes to me far more in the WCC setting. We have tackled there some of the great issues of our torn world, not in the expectation that the churches can solve them but rather that God calls us, within our churches, to be part of the solution. There are plenty of risks involved. A Council of Churches can become self-absorbed, drifting away from its constituency. It can fall over backwards to provide a sounding-board for those who are on the fringes of the church. It is often tempted to take onto the agenda far more great issues than the staff can possibly deal with adequately. And it may at times adopt a tone of superiority which irritates its member churches. All this and more can be said, but this experiment in visible ecumenism has been a vital step towards the wholeness of the church.

These three developments are responses, called by the Spirit of God, to the national imprisonments of the Protestant family and the fracturing of that family into denominations. We have to ask whether either the Catholic or the Protestant pattern has been effective in healing international crises or creating a new atmosphere of trust, or overcoming the deep divisions between North and South, East and West. The answer has to be, not very effective. The two main areas where we would expect an international church to concentrate its prayer and energy are peace and human rights. Here are causes that reach us directly from the bible and from Jesus himself – not that contemporary issues find their solution in a text, but that the whole direction of the biblical witness is towards respect for every human life, the absence of favouritism in God, the call for forgiveness and the hope of community. If we think of the wars that have led to vast pain and waste even since the second world war – South Korea, Vietnam, Cambodia, Biafra, Angola, Morocco, Afghanistan, El Salvador, Nicaragua, the Falklands, Iran/Iraq, Chad, Sri Lanka (an incomplete list) – we realize that the international church has not had much success in preventing the killing. In a good many cases we find nations which have a large Christian component actually providing armaments to the combatants, as though this is a normal exercise in international relations. The United Kingdom now takes pride in this trade. In too many cases the national churches have been captured by nationalism and so support the political desire for dominance. It has often been proposed that Christians should be committed to an end of crusades – the achievement of noble ends by wretched means – but many have still not accepted this. On the credit side we acknowledge the efforts made by churches in the United States to stop the flow of US arms to the *contras* in Nicaragua, a firm position taken with much expert advice. We may wonder whether the Russian Orthodox Church has made, behind the scenes, similar protests about Soviet war-making in Afghanistan.

On human rights, the churches have been active for many years but the record is patchy. Where there has been a concentrated effort over a long period, as there has been with regard to South Africa, there is little doubt that the churches have raised public awareness of the issue and so have helped those who struggle to achieve political equality. It has been noticeable that the impressive weight of the Vatican has helped the human rights struggle in Poland while the WCC has been far more active in South Africa, Chile, Argentina and Central America – the one emphasizing abuses by socialists, the other by right-wing militaristic regimes. We may see this as neatly complementary. But it may be due to a hidden ideology which does not match the theological basis of church action. It is surprising that there has not been greater co-ordination of effort in this field. For example, Amnesty International has shown how people of conviction can campaign on behalf of the multitude of prisoners of conscience. With all its millions of members in every land, why has the church not fulfilled such a ministry with even more powerful effect? Why have we not campaigned incessantly on behalf of Jews in Russia, Amazonian Indians, minorities in Iran, dissidents in Chile? The major reason for this failure is lack of conviction. We easily believe that work for human rights is not for us, not for churches, not the activity of the Holy Spirit.

There is a little of that theological lethargy in most of us. After all, we have plenty of work nearer home. To maintain an effective ministry in a caring church with a sound building and decent balance in the bank is a sufficient struggle for a great many devoted Christians. But the neighbourhood world calls for a neighbourhood church. Who is my neighbour? It is an ancient question and we should not need the electronic media to reveal the answer that the person in need is neighbour whether across the world or next door. National boundaries and national sentiment have very little meaning when life itself is at stake. The Chernobyl cloud did not notice the barbed wire fences, and the Sahel drought respected no national plan. Should God's word of salvation in Christ recognize any greater restriction?

The world crisis of poverty has called for a response from nations and churches, and here the churches have frequently taken the lead, constantly prodding the national conscience by example as well as exhortation. National interest has so far led politicians in power to reject the full weight of this cry of humanity. The cry of self-interest is strong. But by setting up excellent church channels for international aid and using the church networks as distributors and by lobbying politicians, Christians have kept this issue on the political agenda, knowing that only governmental action can effect the major switch in resources which the world needs. This movement across the North/South divide is not only humanitarian. It is deeply religious. It is about our solidarity in pain, our equality before death, and God's unto-death-love for every person. It is Gospel work. This does not mean that the church has only bread to offer, though bread is better than stones; it is that bread and living bread are both God's gift and both needed for life in all its fullness.

CHAPTER TEN

Nation, Church, Kingdom

I

The more tightly we seek to define what we mean by 'nation', the more we expose the difficulties. We can refer to a national government and define the nation as that area of land and that population over which the government has authority. But that tends to collapse when we think of the colonial situation. One government then had authority over a broad mixture of peoples in scattered areas. But this governmental definition still carries a lot of weight and is decisive in the world of politics. Another way of approach is to base the definition on a corporate sense of identity which is affirmed by language, culture and history. It is on such a basis that we have referred to the United Kingdom and the four nations that comprise it. It is a rather shaky basis because it provides no clear limits. Many Welsh people, for example, live in England. Are they Welsh by nationality even unto the tenth generation? A further attempt at definition is through ethnic origin. Then the nation is formed by all who trace their origin to a single source, even if they have lost all association with that source.

Something of this same puzzle occurs in the New Testament. The common word for nations is *ethnoi*, a word never used about the Jewish nation but about others, frequently used of the Greeks, carrying a slightly disparaging note. Jewish worshippers had been long accustomed to the denunciation of the surrounding nations because of their heathen worship, and it was this note of foreign-ness which came through in the New Testament. The other word was *genos* denoting the heredity of belonging, the sense of tribe. It is used in Mark 7.26 about the woman who was 'a Gentile, a Phoenician of Syria by nationality' (NEB); 'by birth' (RSV). Both words are used by Peter in his description of the Christian community as 'a chosen race' and 'a dedicated nation' (I Peter 2.9). The same theme of birth runs through some of Paul's self-descriptions. 'Are they Hebrews? So am I. Israelites? So am I. Abraham's descendants? So am I' (II Cor. 11.22). In Philippians, 'Israelite by race, of the tribe of Benjamin, a Hebrew born and bred' (Phil. 3.5). But the key factor in the Pauline passages is that such a heredity is now counted as nothing, or less than nothing, because of the new 'nationality' given by Christ.

This makes us very reluctant to adopt the ethnic origin emphasis in nationhood. It is always regressive, drawing people back to their genesis and not to either their present situation or their commitment for the future. It is the typical emphasis of the white South African who, by emphasizing tribalism, splits up the black population and consigns them to 'homelands'. This may assure white dominance but raises the awkward question whether the white people are themselves a tribe, and, if so, why are they not on an equal footing with the other tribes to make up one nation? A very clear example of the ethnic emphasis was in Malaysia when ethnic Malay people reacted against Chinese dominance in the commercial life of the nation. A similar and sad case is that of Fiji. There the indigenous Melanesians and the immigrant Indians had lived side by side for many years. Most of the Indians were second or third generation residents. When independence came after a century of British rule, both communities were truly Fijian. They both belonged there and saw their future there. Nearly all the Melanesians were Christians, most of them Methodists. But the Indian side of the population grew to become the majority and, for the first time in 1987, formed part of the ruling party in government. This was the signal for a military coup (the army being almost entirely Melanesian) which expelled from office a democratically elected government and instituted rule by decree on behalf of the Melanesian population. It was an act of racialism. Christianity did not prevent the upsurge of a form of nationalism that was ethnic at base and which now seems destined to place the Indian-origin people at a permanent disadvantage. The seeds of violence have been planted. This is the constant danger and folly of an ethnically based nationalism.

The folly becomes all the plainer in a country of very mixed population. Few people in England today can describe their tribal origins, since mixing has been continuous for so long. So nationalism here can only emphasize the geographical integrity of the realm. 'This sceptred isle' covers the mixture of the population and provides sufficient basis for a unity of concern. But while such a base may be more forward-looking than the racial base, it is still a very limited identity. We are people before we are English or French or Zambian.

It may be that we only find our footing, our secure ground, on the world scene by the national identity we bring. Without that, we belong nowhere. The risk today is that the national belonging becomes so pronounced, so divisive, so self-confident that it destroys the far greater identity of the human family as the children of God, with one Father in heaven and one future on earth. I believe that the experience of nationhood is only one stage in the long process by which humanity learns to live in the world God has given us. If we look at the series – family, village, tribe, city, state, nation – we see an enlarging identity, and there is no reason why this should not be extended. We shall always need our local identities. There is a richness in the diverse cultures which shape our thinking which is not to be traded for a nondescript mishmash. But we are surely learning that the small fragment of humanity to which we belong will only be fulfilled as part of the total pattern.

So, as Christians, we will not invest too great a devotion in the nation state. The nation cannot save us. Government is not all-wise. We can be given a measure of security from enemies and a measure of justice and equality before the law, we can plan the use of precious land, we may even see new towns built and illness attacked with national resources. But the nation cannot save us. The sin which twists our nature is never healed by the intelligent organization of the state. The new blocks of flats easily become networks of petty violence, and all the social security that is provided may fail to cure that basic insecurity of the personality which makes us despair of ourselves and distrust others. The nation cannot save our marriages. In a war it cannot even save our lives. So while we need national identity and national government, we do not invest too much confidence in them. There is a strong case to resist any attempt, however disguised, to pull back the national identity to an ethnic or religious basis on the Old Testament pattern. That would not only be regressive but would threaten peace, as we see in Iran. It could be said that the entry into the Middle East of Israel as a nation, which hallowed its own history and saw divine sanction for its borders, has caused a constant tension which could, if treated only as a human problem, be more readily solved. Nations which become divine are idols. Christians will always be alert for such false assumptions.

Can the nation be saved? 'Make all nations my disciples,' said Jesus in the farewell commission as Matthew recorded it. A nation cannot be saved in the sense of the corporate body being given eternal life and forgiveness and the blessing of the Holy Spirit. Nor can a nation be saved through its ruler, as though the Christian king carries the population with him into blessedness. Can a nation ever fulfil the law of love and care for others as much as for itself? The questions are not simply rhetorical. If we think at all about a Christian mission towards the nation then we need to have some concept of our aim, and if we see a purpose beyond the conversion of individuals then we need some view of the good society. This is not to belittle conversion. It remains for ever at the core of Christian witness. But it is not the whole, for the evidence of history is that all manner of evils can continue in the social order even when a majority of the population holds firmly to Christian faith. Individualist religion does not of itself solve corporate problems.

It is too easy to think of a good society as one that is good for Christians, that secures our freedom and favours our morality and respects our institutions. That may be part of the answer, but is surely not the whole. The world does not exist for our sake. Rather we have to look at ways in which this powerful organ of social life can contribute to the development of the world towards the pattern willed by God. This means freedom for our faith, but for other faiths too. I believe it means movement away from extremes of competition (which divides people) and enforced equality (which reduces people to units in the system). It involves a system of justice which is unaffected by race, class or ability to pay. The Gospel would also lead us to expect that a good society protects the weak, the handicapped, the children, and gives them first place in social concern. On the other side, a good society limits the exercise of power by the strong and wealthy, so that no forms of slavery are possible and personal greed cannot hijack the resources of the country. Further, in all its confrontations with other nations, it will go to great lengths to deal in negotiation rather than resort to force. These are very personal assessments and many others have been attempted. The nation can be saved from serving evil if its major policies are directed in such ways as these. It is not that nation states can build God's Kingdom or any Utopia. There is no 'steady state' of social righteousness in this world. But the Christian calling can mean for us that the social direction is towards this world of justice and peace and creativity which we all need if we are to live life to the full.

II

Through the gift of the Holy Spirit the first Christians broke out from the restrictions of the tribal or ethnic faith, were freed from one cultural view and were able to minister to their world. The apostolic church had a world view. In the New Testament, the word 'church' is used in two main ways. It means a local assembly of Christians, either in a house or in a town. The word *ekklesia* is used some 77 times in this way, 42 as a singular and 35 as a plural noun. It also means the entire Christian community, the whole body of disciples at all times and places; it is used 24 times in that way. It is never used to mean either one particular stream of theology or the Christians of one province or tribe. These two are very common current meanings, but the New Testament evidence suggests that neither can be treated as necessary for the truth of the Gospel and the way of Christ.

The intermediate levels of church, between the local and the universal, are pragmatic rather than essential to faith. We need them for the sake of effective sharing between Christians, for the aid of the poor in the world, for the provision of specialist services, for fellowship, for public influence, and for the careful ordering of ministries. We cannot fulfil, in a wholly local, congregational way all that God calls us to do. One point which has been at issue between denominations is whether the diocese and its bishop is the 'local church' in the New Testament sense and therefore a theological requirement. Although we can see a line of development from the apostolic ministry, the gathering of presbyters around the president and the recognition of apostolic authority, that line cannot be used as a theological defence today. For during the middle ages the area of oversight of the bishops in Western Europe was not primarily a religious matter at all. It was to do with politics, wealth, noble allies and conflict. The position of the bishop became analogous to that of a prince, and so, in parts of Europe, those two titles were run together. The diocese became far too large for proper pastoral care, and so the bishop became a distant figure, far removed from the local worshipping life of Christians. We live with the medieval legacy. Diocesan bishops still have far too many local churches and ministers under their care, so that they have to fly from one to another for quick engagements. That is not the local church in New Testament terms. If we are ever to receive the bishop, as pastoral president, in the churches of the Reformed tradition, it will surely be on a much more local scale, so that the person is truly at home in the congregations and can effectively lead their missionary witness. There was an interesting moment in the English Covenant debate in 1980 when Methodism had to decide whether, if the Covenant went ahead, its bishops would be the district chairmen or the circuit superintendents. The choice went to the former (with areas larger than a diocese) when the creative move might well have been to urge the latter, and so to help the

Church of England re-think its path out of the medieval legacy. The Roman Catholic church has been particularly anxious to invest the diocese with great theological weight, and here again I believe a fresh look is required if we are to discover the meaning of 'local church' for today.

The national level of church life is not an aspect of the theological essence of what the church is called to be. It exists in the Protestant and Orthodox world as a Christian response to the rise of nation states. It has validity so long as it carries a missionary purpose, revealing on the national scene the word of reconciliation and hope, cross and resurrection. It is a word of challenge because the cross always stands in judgment of those powers which belittle human life. National churches therefore are uncomfortable friends of national leaders, and this will apply whatever the ideological trend of the nation, for in every human political system there are destructive tendencies. In some places the immediate trend of the political community seems close to the church's thinking, and Zimbabwe and Nicaragua are current examples. But even there I believe that faithfulness in the church will mean the exposure of abuses which do occur when political opponents are deprived of their full rights as citizens. In places where there is no permitted political opposition, the watchman function of the church becomes very significant. There is also a word of encouragement and solidarity. The church does not exist solely to point to what belittles human life but to stimulate all that makes for human fulfilment. Yet strangely we are very long on criticism, very short on praise. When, for example, countries in Western Europe are able to subordinate purely national interests to a wider objective, then the courage of their leaders deserves Christian support. This does not happen often. When it does, there is a movement towards a world community. When a small nation, like the Republic of Ireland, contributes fully to United Nations' international peace-keeping, the church should be able to express thanksgiving, because influence for peace is no longer confined to the great powers. When a national government in New Zealand can join Pacific islanders in rejecting all nuclear weapons, the churches may well express gratitude for a vision realized.

Challenge and encouragement are two expressions of the Christian critique of public policy. The third voice is that of faith. The national witness to Christ must have this clear reminder that this is God's world and we are his people, that life is not confined to the visible world, that God seeks to redeem all human life and that everyone, without exception, is precious to God. This faith does not make us good politicians, for we may be quite unskilled at that craft, but it compels us to remain unsatisfied with all power-seeking processes which fail to recognize the power of God. We might sing with the psalmist:

Man's days are like the grass;
he blossoms like the flowers of the field:
a wind passes over them, and they cease to be,
and their place knows them no more.
But the Lord's love never fails those who fear him;
his righteousness never fails their sons and their grandsons
who listen to his voice and keep his covenant,
who remember his commandments and obey them.
The Lord has established his throne in heaven,
his kingly power over the whole world (Ps. 103.15–19).

And we might dare to echo Isaiah in every parliament house,

Why, to him nations are but drops from a bucket,
no more than moisture on the scales (Is. 40.15).

Faith looks beyond the appearances of power to the finality of God.

But how can the church speak with these voices? We know how weak is the body of Christ, how fractured it is. Even when the church is assembled in its national synod or conference it remains a body without power, able to act only through goodwill and often swayed by fear of losing support. And when the national church appears at its most glorious, with the processions of clergy in gold and white and purple, in the most splendid of shrines with trumpeters in the organ loft and dazzling plate on the altar, even then the church is weak. It is but a voice pleading with the human heart, a finger pointing towards the Lord, a cup of wine, a smile of confidence when death is near, a companionship in tears, a whispered prayer. It is also, God forgive us, a frequent self-concern, a love of small arguments, a go-it-alone mentality and a perverse assurance that, because our faith is focused in historical events, so we should sanctify our own history. We need to be modest both because we are only servants of the Lord, and because we know what poor quality servants we are. But we still point towards the wonder of the king and his kingly rule.

III

It is that understanding of the Kingdom which draws together our experience of the church and our life as citizens in powerful modern states. The phrases 'Kingdom of God' and 'Kingdom of Heaven' are the special language of Jesus. This was the text of his life as well as his sermon. Because human understanding of the purpose of eternal God will always be elementary, we are given parables of the Kingdom, pictures of different facets of a great reality. The rule of God, in the gospels, is both present and to come. It is both internal in the heart and a way of life for the world. Salvation in the Christian sense is that healing of our nature which brings us into a realm of forgiveness and new love. It can be described in a host of ways. We can speak of liberation, of the new creation, of baptism, of the power of the cross. But, for me, one of the most evocative descriptions is that given by the apostle John in his first letter.

> It was there from the beginning; we have heard it; we have seen it with our own eyes; we looked upon it, and felt it with our own hands, and it is of this we tell. Our theme is the word of life. This life was made visible; we have seen it and bear our testimony; we here declare to you the eternal life which dwelt with the Father and was made visible to us. What we have seen and heard we declare to you, so that you and we together may share in a common life, that life which we share with the Father and his Son Jesus Christ (I John 1.1–3).

The passion of first-hand experience runs through this paragraph, the phrases tumbling out one after the other, and we note that none other than the first group of disciples could write like this. However vivid the spiritual experience of the saints, the original eye-witness is unrepeatable. The last sentence is a key to understanding what salvation-history is all about. John witnesses to the person of Christ so that others far beyond the immediate circle may share in a common life which actually is divine life. This common life (*koinonia*) is our joyful relationship with our Creator, made possible by the earthly life of Jesus. We know God through Jesus and our faith joins us to him, faith which God himself inspires in us. The church is that common life made visible throughout the world. As we share in a baptism or eat the holy meal, as we pray together, as we serve one another's needs, and campaign for another's rights, as we make companions out of strangers and open our doors to the lonely, so the common life is lived. As Christians exclude one another from the Lord's table, so the common life is denied. That is why unity and mission always belong together, for there is not only a Gospel to be preached but a life to be shared. That life is God's eternity in our time, the forever which entered the world in a man, and which we acknowledge every time we pray. It is that life which is the indestructibility of the church. Much of the edifice of the church may indeed disappear, but the promise of Christ is our assurance that even the gates of hell do not overpower the common life 'which we share with the Father and his Son Jesus Christ'. The church points towards the Kingdom of God through all the many forms of life-expression which are opened up to the world in worship, celebration, sacrificial giving and the continuous service of the needy.

Yet even the church at its best is only one dimension of human society. The church is not the sum total of human experience, but it exists to express the divine will for the whole world. Is that 'common life' the purpose of God for all? The Gospel says yes. And the contemporary world scene tells us yes. There will be no ultimate peace, in its deepest sense, without a common life for all the nations in which there is both mutual respect and a sharing of gifts. The nation can only serve the great purposes of God if there is a common life for its own people – an identity and a burden-bearing and a responsibility for one another – and participation in the wider family of humankind. On the hard road to such a goal there are very powerful forces to be met, as we all know to our cost. The tight self-interest of the state, its *Realpolitik* mentality that power is the only ultimate right, constantly appeals to our unredeemed nature. Our obsession with continual economic growth in the West, whatever this might cost to people in poor countries drained of their raw materials, and however futile to the human spirit, that obsession has become a voters' test of all political parties. Always the realization of the Kingdom is delayed by sin, which may appear like the four horsemen bearing today's names of hunger, war, oppression and despair. It is in that struggle that the nations of the world have a duty towards God, inescapable, permanent, often unacknowledged, costly, requiring tolerance and not absolutism. Church truly serves nation when it promotes faithfulness in this calling of God.

But I believe the 'common life' has a yet wider reference. The biblical vision of creation reveals to us a community of both natural world and humanity; it is all one creation. This very basic unity has become overlaid by successive religious perceptions. The earliest was that human beings were masters of the natural world; that it existed for them; they were to subdue it. This may indeed have been a very appropriate response when the world was relatively empty and dark chaos surrounded precarious human habitation. To make an orderly space was a primary need. This attitude was succeeded by concepts of stewardship. Humanity was then not the master but only a guardian, gardener, steward, caring for the earth. Our duty was to gain an adequate profit from the earth, but in such a way that the earth was improved rather than destroyed.

Today we are called to move beyond that vision. We now live in a very crowded world when the demands made on the resources of nature are accelerating. There is a note of mastery in our modern skills. There is stewardship, too, as we accept responsibility before God. But beyond that there is a unity of humankind and nature which is becoming plainer every day. We are part of the natural world. We, too, are affected by the tides of climate and fertility. The air we breathe is part of us, and if we pollute the water supply then we all suffer. The purpose of God is the re-creation of the world, restoring all to that common life in which obedience to his way assures life, and disobedience is the sure route to death.

We die alone. So the individualist European reflects on the personal road to God. At the end neither family nor nation nor church accompanies us on the last journey. Bound up in our self, no one can intervene. 'What I do with my own solitariness' is one definition of religion. But it is not so. The way of the Kingdom is a way of a common life which abolishes the barriers between your heart and mine, between gangs and parties and classes of people. Our personal journey is then never alone. It is within the company of all who are pilgrims with us, of every nation and language, of every variety of human culture. The diversity of the human family and our distinctiveness within it, is not the issue. It is how we live a family life and not a family death that is the crux for humanity. Are we there at that point with prayer and passion and the utter conviction that God is good and has poured out for the world all that is needed for salvation?

A NOTE ON ETHNIC CHURCHES

In the light of the barrier-breaking commission of the church, how do we face the large number of ethnically based churches? They mainly occur in two forms:

(a) where there are many temporary expatriates living, for example, a Scots church in Paris, a Samoan church in California, a Dutch church in London, an English church in Delhi, an American church in Manila.

(b) where national boundaries have moved to include a different population (as Hungarian speakers in Romania), or where there is a permanent and sizeable population of very distinctive origin (as Tamils in Malaysia).

The first comment must be that there is no such thing as an ethnic Christian church. It is a contradiction in terms, since the reality of Christ means the breaking down of all ethnic limitations on the fellowship of his disciples. This is one of the central defects of the apartheid system, and the reason why many people call it heretical.

But we can recognize culturally identified churches. That is, churches whose ethos, worship style, language and corporate activity relate to the culture of one group. There is much support for the indigenous elements in worship, what truly grows out of local tradition. So such churches cannot be ruled out of order, *provided they are not ethnic* and thus exclusive.

It is not always an easy distinction, and some of the positive aspects to look for are as follows:

(i) When a population group is in a small minority, particularly if it is composed of first generation migrants, there is a great need to establish confidence, cherish customs and language and so keep an identity as a group. Many congregations have focused on this purpose. The risk is to hold this position too long, for generations, when the urgent need has long departed.

(ii) A key factor is whether the culturally-focused church is a backward-looking or forward-looking influence. To proclaim the Gospel of new creation must always be a forward-looking activity. So if the church is largely concerned to lead people back to the homeland, to memories far away, to nostalgia, then it is unlikely to serve the urgent tasks of discipleship.

(iii) It is right to ask how this group relates to the other churches of the country. Sometimes the 'chaplaincy' type of congregation (for reasons both good and bad) has little to do with neighbouring churches. It sees all its links 'back home'. The language problem may be part of the reason for this. But it may also be escapism from the calling to witness together to the Lord in the locality. The question, therefore, to put is whether there are growing local relationships with other Christians, mutual trust and co-operation, so that we may progress towards the unity of 'all in each place'.

(iv) In some places there is a risk of empire-building by the home church. That is, a conscious effort to avoid the local links mentioned in (iii) above, so that all the resources of the 'daughter churches' may be directed back home. This has happened quite frequently with Pacific islanders' groups in the United States. It indicates a very restricted vision of the church and is probably founded on money contributions from the more affluent economy.

(v) Where there is a large, settled community with its own identifiable style of church life, like the Greek Orthodox in Australia, we have to ask rather different questions. Since the creation of good community relations is vital for both peace and justice, how is church life contributing? Does the church distinctiveness grow out of theology or language or taste or habit? If we seek diversity of culture in one national community, is there openness to other churches, mutual understanding, and full co-operation in social enterprise? Does the church encourage the learning of a common language?

It is not always easy to press such questions, since both home church and distant offspring are frequently satisfied with the status quo. Help can be given if all are invited to share in local and regional councils of churches. Also, if the large national churches can offer friendship and a welcoming umbrella, this is a very productive beginning.

This is, indeed, the other side of the equation, illustrated in the English experience. It is a critical time for old-established churches when immigrants arrive. What welcome do churches offer? How open are they to a different style of worship or special language services? The English churches did far too little in the 1950s and 1960s to receive Caribbean Christians, with the result that there was added impetus to forming black congregations and quite separate denominations. This is in contrast to the experience in New Zealand when, in the 1950s, Polynesians were settling in considerable numbers, particularly in Auckland. The welcome from the churches was warm, accommodation was offered, lay people gave their services in many ways, for example to help run Sunday schools. The result has been that the great majority of the islanders have remained within the main-line churches, providing an enlivening presence. To maintain diversity in unity takes hard work and spiritual understanding, but is a key ministry in our plural societies.

A NAME, BUT NOT BABEL

We need a name that rings around the world.
Yes, this people is tough, great fighters, never give in.
This people is all music and passion, poets of the hills.
This people is puffed up like a kitten
all arched back and fur erect before a mongrel.
And this people, so cunning with their hands,
tireless craftsmen, their fame travels.
And that people, watch your purse,
they're sharp, they sell sand to the Saudis.
Give us a name. Salute our flag.
Love our green hills and the spires of village churches.
Defend our way of life. Give us a name.

> Why did you, Palestinian Jew,
> only work for God's Kingdom?
> No praise from you for a greater Israel,
> a mightier Herod, a more golden Jerusalem.

It's a strange pain-love, this feeling for my country.
So much makes me ashamed; yet pride still lingers.
Help me rejoice when there is something to be proud of,
some generosity of spirit, some offering to the needy,
discoveries of justice and riches of hope,
open doors for those fleeing oppression,
and the best care for all our children.

> Don't call us Babel, Lord,
> Don't scatter us like worthless pebbles,
> But fashion us and shape us
> so that we may be one piece of colour
> in your great mosaic of common life
> which bears the name, Image of God.